YOU ARE A
New Creation

YOU ARE A
New Creation

MAUREEN SCHULER, PSY.D.

MainSpring Books

Copyright © 2020 by Maureen Schuler, PSY.D.

All rights reserved. No part of this publication may be reproduced, distributed, or transmitted in any form or by any means, including photocopying, recording, or other electronic or mechanical methods, without the prior written permission of the author, except in the case of brief quotations embodied in critical reviews and certain other noncommercial uses permitted by copyright law.

Printed in the United States of America
ISBN 978-1-947352-98-8 (paperback)
ISBN 978-1-64133-637-6 (hardback)
ISBN 978-1-947352-99-5 (ebook)
Library of Congress Control Number: 2020923024

MainSpring Books
5901 W. Century Blvd
Suite 750
Los Angeles, CA, US, 90045

www.mainspringbooks.com

TABLE OF CONTENTS

Ancestry 7

My Mother's Influence 11

The Active Community 19

My Truth 27

A New Path 31

The Chalice 42

The Faith That We Share 44

Living Our Baptismal Sharing in the Priesthood of Christ 51

The Threshold of Eternity 57

To Be Shared 62

That We Might Give Glory to God 65

PREFACE

For fourteen or more years, I have read, pondered over, meditated upon, and, frankly, questioned the words of God the Father to St. Catherine of Siena.

As for any assault against yourself, consider that my will permits it to prove virtue in you and in my other servants. And assume that the offender does such a thing as an instrument commissioned by me. For often such a person's intention is good; there is no one who can judge the hidden heart.

More about that in pages to come. However, changing the perspective from, "God allows this for my own good," to "This is God's work, his *design*, for the creation within me of his divine image," has altered the experience for me as unimaginably beautiful rather than horribly painful.

And looking back over a lifetime whose meaning was inscrutable to me has now become an awe in spiring story of God's work of creation in my life.

It is also my hope that this writing will also be a manifestation of the beauty of God's creation. That beauty is shown in many ways: it is the inspiration of every artist whose very being is so struck by a loveliness that he or she beholds in nature that the artist is compelled to attempt to capture that beauty and to convey it in paintings, in music, in every medium, including the written word.

And so my hope is that this writing will be for the glory of God.

INTRODUCTION

I begin this writing with the hope that "in all things, may God be glorified." It is also my hope that this will not be so much a life history as an illustration of God's continuing work in creation.

I believe that this a wonderful story. Not a wonderful story about myself, but a wonderful story about God. It is no glitch in reflection that the readings for the Easter Liturgy include the creation account. God did not stop the work of creation when, on the seventh day, he rested. We are all—each one of us—the handiwork of God's continuing work of creation. The picture of God's creation is vast. Genesis tells us that God made man in his own image. That is not some kind of mold of humanity; rather, in the infinite beauty of God, each soul is created to reflect some aspect of the wonder and beauty of God.

Each life is designed by God to grow in the reflection of himself for which he created it.

Every person, circumstance, event is part of the divine design.

George Weigel, in his book *Roman Pilgrimage* quotes the Dominican, Bede Jarrett, in the understanding of embracing the will of God:

This life of ours…is a gift from God. It is not of our choosing. It comes to us by his choice. Since it is of his choosing, it is of his designing. We neither made ourselves nor can we manage ourselves as we like, nor manage the life that comes to us. For that reason, we can take a most hopeful view of life…(For) the thought that it is his gift and after his design gives us courage. If to this remembrance of God's creatorship, we add the mystery of the Resurrection, we shall take even larger draughts of hope, for not only life, but life's triumph lies entirely in the hands of God.

And that is not just for our realization of our own call to cooperate with God's creative activity in our own lives. It also bids us to *realize* (not just think about) the aspect of the divine image in each person with whom we come in contact. To comprehend this work of God has been, for me, a personal struggle. I imagined that I had to do some kind of mind control and build up a habit of reflecting on the presence of God in others. I was chagrined, thinking that I just didn't have it in me to do what so many spiritual books told me that I was supposed to do.

But it becomes a whole lot more spontaneous to realize that creation is ongoing. To see the "bigger picture" is enlightening. In addition, it clarifies another long-standing problem that I have had.

For fourteen or more years I have read, pondered over, meditated upon, and frankly, questioned the words of God the Father to St. Catherine of Siena. "As for any assault against yourself, consider that my will permits it to prove virtue in you and in my other servants. And assume that the offender does such a thing as an instrument commissioned by me. For often such a person's intention is good; there is no one who can judge the hidden heart." More about that in pages to come.

However, changing the perspective from, "God allows this for my own good," to: this is God's work, His design, for the creation within me of His divine image, has altered the experience for me as unimaginably beautiful rather than horribly painful. And, looking back over a lifetime whose meaning was inscrutable to me has now become an awe-inspiring story of God's work of creation in my life.

It is also my hope that this writing will also be a manifestation of the beauty of God's creation. That beauty is shown in many ways—it is the inspiration of every artist whose very being is so struck by a loveliness that he or she beholds in nature that the artist is compelled to attempt to capture that beauty, and to convey it in paintings, in music, in every medium, including the written word.

And, so my hope is that this writing will be for the glory of God.

"You are a new creation" (12 Cor. 5:17). Cooperating with God in the designs that he has for our lives allows him to make of our souls the eternal beauty for which we were created. It is not because we are good, learned, or even worthwhile, but because we belong to the God who loves us, that the design planned for us by God in some strangely magnificent way forms us into a new creation.

ANCESTRY

I begin the journey back to my ancestry as far as I know it. It begins with my great, great grandfather on my father's side of the family.

The name that we know him by is Bartholomew Schuler. However, it is unlikely that this was his original name. The surname Schuler has been denied by the family lore, as will be seen subsequently. If, as you will come to understand, he was intent on changing his surname, why would he have kept his given name? That suggests that his name was not Bartholomew or Schuler.

We have a timeline for him.

1776: (or 1774) Born in Bohemia, Austria.

1793: Began seven years of service in the Austrian Army. (History records that when Napoleon defeated the Austrian Army, he took over 23,000 men from the Austrian Army. That might explain how Bartholomew came to be in Napoleon's army.)

1800: Fought in Napoleon's army in the Egyptian campaign.

1810: He and a companion (Stephen Baudendistle) escaped from Napoleon's army and went to Switzerland. They subsequently went to Bohemia where they worked for a wealthy woodsman.

1816: Immigrated to the United States as an indentured servant to his woodsman employer from Bohemia. It is at this point that lore has it that he changed his name to Schuler, the name of the captain of the ship.

However, the ship's manifold gives the captain's surname as "Schultz" (maybe close enough).

1816: Married Rosina Schaller (who had been born in Switzerland) to whom he had been betrothed while in Bohemia.

1818: His sponsor, on his deathbed, released him from indenture and gave Bartholomew, his wife, and infant son each one dollar.

? Moved to Venango County, Pennsylvania.

? Moved Loretto, Pennsylvania.

1826: Moved to Fayetteville, Brown County, Ohio.

1836: With Joseph Bareck (Birch) and Stephen Baudendistle (Baurntish) (it appears that either spelling or handwriting was unpredictable at this time) entered land near Jasper, Indiana.

1837: Settled his family in Jasper, Indiana (apparently leaving someone to take care of the farm in Fayetteville, because that remained in the family, as will be seen later).

1854: Died in Jasper, Indiana, age seventy-eight.

1866: His widow Rosina (Rose) died in Jasper.

It would seem that it might be because of his many travels that he was called a gypsy.

Documentation about Bartholomew is interesting.

The first documentation is found in a book that is no longer in print entitled *The Cross in the Wilderness*. On page 8 of that book, it states:

Then one fine morning, Fenwick, now bishop, turned from his desk in Cincinnati to face two women and two men, Bartelmy Schuler and Stephen Baudendistle, Bohemians, with their wives. Schuler and Baundistl had been runaway soldiers from Napoleons army in Egypt; refugees in Switzerland, they had married into a Bohemian family and, to get across to America had sold themselves for seven years to a ship captain; liberated in New York, they had started westward down the Ohio.

The book continues:

"Go out to the lands that are mine in Brown County," said the bishop reading thrift, honesty, religion in their weary faces. "Cut down some trees and build yourselves cabins. All you can raise upon the land is yours to keep. Build me a church and I'll send you a priest to help you save your souls."

Records from Indiana do not mention the two men as having been runaways from Napoleon's army. Perhaps the men decided that it was best to omit that from their stories. It hardly seems likely that they would have freely given the information to Bishop Fenwick if it that was not the truth.

Looking upon this history, not as happenstance or the wanderings of a person who has met with multiple failures in his attempt to provide a livelihood for his family and himself but the work of divine creation, it unfolds to be a marvel of God's continuing creation. Nothing was happening by chance, all by Divine Providence, all forming the divine image.

Just looking at the facts, here was a man who was willing to keep going, even literally. He took the opportunity to immigrate to America, perhaps driven by fear of possible punishment for "having run away" from Napoleon's army while in Egypt.

He was unsuccessful in Pennsylvania in his attempts at farming, but he traveled to Ohio. He was a man of faith as shown by offering his services to Bishop Fenwick of Cincinnati. His Catholic faith is noted in the history of Dubois County, Indiana.

The faith continued through subsequent generations as witnessed to by my grandfather Julius Schuler, who, when he lost the Schuler farm in Fayetteville due to swine cholera wiping out all of the pigs, moved to Norwood, Ohio, to become the janitor for St. Matthews Church, school, rectory, and convent. He used his love for beauty in planting the loveliest church landscaping of any church in the area. He built a stage with backdrops for the school children's performances.

He wrote charming poetry, composing in rhyme a class prophecy naming each graduating eighth grader and read at a dinner that he gave each year for the graduates.

In addition, he and my father, both of whom had fine tenor voices, sang in the men's choir of St. Matthew Church. (As an aside, there were no women's choirs. It was against church law for women to even be in the choir loft, the church sanctuary as well.)

From Bartholomew's line of descent, his son Bartholomew Jr. married Crescentia Baudendistel (presumably Stephen's daughter). Their son, John Bartholomew, married Ann Dirvin who died some time later, leaving John Bartholomew with two sons and two daughters.

He remarried in 1880 to Jane Kirskadden with whom he had six more children, among which was my grandfather, Julius Schuler. It appears that John Bartholomew was the owner and farmer of the Fayetteville farm, which then became the responsibility of his oldest son from his second marriage, Julius. My grandfather recounted that he had brothers and sisters whom he had never met, because they had left home before he was born.

In all that I remember about my grandfather, there was a deep commitment to the church. This is not about genetics. It is more about a heritage of faith and the values transmitted in living out that faith.

MY MOTHER'S INFLUENCE

My mother's genealogy is only traced by lore and only goes back three generations. That is because the story begins with my great grandfather. He arrived in America as a stowaway aboard a ship from Germany. When he was discovered, he was befriended by an apparently affluent passenger who paid his fare and gave him one dollar. There is no information about how he made his way to Oldenburg, Indiana, but so he did.

The story picks up when his son, my grandfather, Clement Kessing, at the age of twelve, is given one dime and put on a train going from Oldenburg, Indiana, to Cincinnati, Ohio. The dime was to pay for his trolley fare from the train station to Lower Price Hill, Cincinnati. Lower Price Hill differentiates from Upper Price Hill, a more affluent community. My grandfather was apprenticed to a tailor.

After serving his apprenticeship and, I presume, being hired as a tailor, he met and married Catherine Scholueke. They had two sons, Frank and Al, and three daughters, Helen, Mary (my mother), and Marcy. (They had at least one child who did not survive). In 1904, my grandfather moved the family to a newly built home in Norwood, a suburb of Cincinnati. My grandfather then worked for Raab Brothers, a family-owned tailoring shop. Later, he would work for Mabley & Carew, a department store. I do not know if Frank and Al were still living at home at that time of the move to

Norwood; considering the family history of boys leaving home at the age of twelve, it was possible that they were not. I do know that both boys settled in Norwood when they returned from the First World War.

I never knew my grandmother Catherine as she died before I was born. My mother loved her dearly. My grandfather never quite got over her loss. One thing that spoke very poignantly of his pain was that after he retired, Grandpa Kessing began to attend daily mass and receive Holy Communion daily. This was significant because my grandmother had been a daily communicant in spite of my grandfather's disapproval, evidently from a Jansenistic background. He appeared to deeply regret that he had discouraged his beloved wife from her daily assistance at mass and daily reception of Holy Communion.

My grandfather Kessing manifested unselfish charity. After his death, exploration of the attic in the homestead revealed a box in which he had kept a record of every man for whom, during the Depression, he had made a suit, free of charge. The records were identified by a code, not names. Only my grandfather knew the key to the code. Many had not repaid my grandfather. He had never mentioned the unpaid debts. In such steadfast charity, my grandfather gave witness to his participation in the new creation inaugurated by our Lord.

The younger man is my grandfather.

My mother affirmed her father's goodness as she lovingly remembered that her father never raised his voice, never showed anger or irritation; Grandpa always presented calmness and strength. His life from the age of twelve was other directed.

I always knew that my grandfather loved me, loved my brother, and all of his children. He reflected the love of God the Father for his children.

My own parents lived in troubled times. They had World War I, the Depression, World War II, the aftermath of World War II. There were always struggles. Their lives were hard. I think that their best years were realized after Jack and I grew up and left home, although my brother did not leave home until he was thirty years old. This was not for want of trying. He put a lot of energy into looking for a spouse. But he did achieve that goal. And then Mom and Dad could give full attention to each other. They grew together in their faith as they became devoted and active in the Franciscan Third Order. It was a beautiful and inspiring sight to witness their love for one another grow. They had always been tremendous examples of faith. Mother took my brother and I to daily mass. She gave us a deep love for prayer, a strong devotion to the Blessed Sacrament, to the saints, and trust in our guardian angels. She also gave us a love for learning.

My father was an unfailing example of steadfastness, unwavering fidelity to all that being Catholic meant. They were amazing examples of a steadfast faith throughout disappointments and hardships.

For as long as I can remember, the Catholic faith was the cornerstone of our lives. I remember clearly the day of my first communion. I had been told that whatever I asked for when I received our Lord for the first time, I would receive. I initially planned to ask for a puppy. I did so long for a puppy. But I remembered that my mother told me that she was afraid of dogs, and puppies grew into dogs. So I decided not to ask for a puppy. But what could I ask for that would make everyone happy? "I know," I said to myself as I was walking toward church, "I would ask to be a nun." I was quite sure that my mother would like that, and I thought my father would, too. As for my brother, I didn't think he would care one way or the other.

That was all well and good, but I really grew tired of everyone saying, "Maureen is going to be a nun when she grows up." So, thinking to put a stop to such talk, I said, "No, I really want to be a nurse." My mother quickly said, "Oh, you can do both. You can be a nun and a nurse." It wasn't that I had given up all thoughts of entering the convent, but I didn't want to give up the freedom of making my own decision.

Something new emerged in high school. I had been invited to join a Catholic action group.

This was a movement in the 1940s, I think, to deepen the faith of teenagers.

Our moderator taught us the prayer of meditation, and I became enamored of prayer. And in the summer between my sophomore and junior years, several of the nuns asked me to help them as they taught religion as a summer mission at a country church. My job was to teach the preschool children. I was a horrible flop at that.

However, the priest who came with us and offered mass was a professor at the local major seminary. I don't remember exactly how it was arranged, but he became my spiritual director. He was a wonderful holy, learned, humble man who some years later entered Our Lady of Gethsemane Trappist Monastery in Kentucky. Throughout my junior and senior years of high school, he gave me direction and books to read beginning with St. Therese of Lisieux's *Story of a Soul* and St. Francis de Sales's *Devout Life* and moving to works by Dom Marmion and Garrigou-Lagrange.

I so loved prayer and spiritual reading that I determined that I wanted to enter a cloistered community. When I shared with the sister-in-charge of our Catholic action group, she told me about the cloistered Passionist nuns. Her brother was a Passionist priest.

I made a retreat with the Passionist nuns at St. Joseph Monastery, which at that time was in Owensboro, Kentucky. Of course, I wanted to enter immediately, but I was gently but firmly persuaded to finish high school first.

In my senior year of high school, I had a striking experience, the like of which would emerge later in my life. It was the experience of not being believed in.

I was my school's representative in an archdiocesan essay contest in which participants wrote an essay on a designated subject and delivered the essay orally to a panel of judges. The topic was the church.

I did not win the contest and our school principal, who was there, enquired of the judges who had evaluated the contestants why I had not won. The answer was, "She had to have help in writing that essay. No teenager could have written that." The principal relayed that to my mother who told me what had been said.

I had written every word of that essay, and I just didn't know what to think about their comment. They had said that it wasn't possible, but it was exactly what happened. I thought how was it that they said that I couldn't have written what I really did write, entirely by myself, with no help whatsoever. This was what I experienced as a sort preamble of what was to come in later years, not being believed in.

But my concern at that time was preparing to enter a cloistered community. One of the reasons why I chose a cloistered community was because I loved learning, and I was surrendering the opportunity of a college education as a sacrifice. I learned soon enough that I would have more sacrifices to offer.

The time that I spent in the cloister was painful. What contributed to the difficulties that I experienced was that I was in the midst of a group who all came from a rural background—the same rural background, the same rural area, the same parish. They were comfortable in the chores of cooking, cleaning, gardening. Unfortunately, I had none of these skills, and I failed at all tasks assigned to me, except one. I could type the address stickers to be attached to the boxes of hosts to be sent to neighboring parishes. The job of baking and cutting hosts for the Eucharist was assigned to the novitiate. I failed in being able to bake the hosts and being to cut the hosts.

Then I had another problem. When being corrected, we were required to kneel to receive the correction. My problem was that I had trouble in figuring out when I was being corrected. I would kneel when I was not being corrected and fail to kneel when I was being corrected. I was corrected quite a lot, so you would think that I would have gotten it straight. In fact, I was the only one in the whole community to be given the penance of having to eat a meal on the floor.

While I must have done something very bad to have been given such a penance, I cannot, for the life of me, remember what it was. I do remember the awkwardness of trying to balance a bowl of soup in one hand while attempting to spoon it with the other while kneeling.

About six months into my year of postulancy, I began having pains, which were diagnosed as appendicitis. Mother Superior decided that I should return home to have the surgery as the hospital at that time in Owensboro was not as equipped as hospitals in larger cities. So I went home for the surgery and recuperation. Upon return to the cloister, Mother Superior advised me that I would now be required to complete one more entire year of being a postulant.

I was admitted into the novitiate then, given the name Sister Marie Therese of the Child Jesus of the Holy Face.

In the retreat before profession, I told the novice mistress that I didn't think that I should be professed. She responded by saying that I should be professed because when I went home for the appendectomy, the nuns had prayed that I would not return, but if I did return, I would be given the name Sister Marie Therese of the Child Jesus of the Holy Face. Since I returned, that seemed to mean to the nuns that I was meant to stay.

At some point, I can't remember exactly when this was. I became so tense about not being able to get things straight that I was unable to chant the divine office. My voice just wouldn't work. So I asked to be a lay sister instead of a choir sister. Of course, there was a major problem in that decision. I had absolutely no knowledge of kitchen work. My mother never let me help in the kitchen; for what you must suspect, I had no skills in the area. She didn't want me spoiling the meal in my ineptitude. So when given the responsibility of taking care of a pressure cooker filled with jars of beans and the timer indicating that the beans were finished, I remembered that I had seen the cook releasing the steam from the pressure cooker before removing the jars from the pressure cooker. Keeping silent, I attempted to remove the jars of beans from the pressure cooker, only to have jars of beans explode, burning my arms and face, and I presume covering the ceiling, floor, and the whole area with beans and glass. I went into shock, I suppose, because I remember telling everyone that I was all right. However, I was taken to the hospital by ambulance. About that stay, I'll just remark that not all doctors are kind.

From that point it, was even more downhill. I can only say that I was physically miserable, and I presume that I was diagnosed as having psychological problems. So the bishop's decision was that I needed to leave the community. My parents came to get me and take me home. My mother asked the superior if she thought that I might ever become a nun. Mother Superior said, "Perhaps in years to come." I presume that I was considered to be very unfit.

My parents had sold our home several years before that and now lived with my brother in an apartment, so there were tight quarters. My father set about putting some weight on me, as I had been very overweight when I entered the community and lost over a hundred pounds while there.

I quickly regained my health. My father, who worked in the farm equipment department of Sears and Roebuck got me a secretarial job in Sears Warehouse. This was where the truckers congregated. In the first week, I was reduced to tears by the way one trucker spoke to me. The manager of the warehouse took him to task and one of the truckers, a very imposingly large fellow, happened to be engaged to a girl with whom I had gone to school. He became my guardian angel. And no more tears were shed.

As I experienced myself as returning to normal, I began thinking of joining another religious community, but an active one. An active community pursues work outside of the convent, whereas cloistered communities have their members involved in occupations within the confines of the monastery. At least, that was the way it was "back in the day." Probably why I was attracted to that particular community, the Passionist Nuns, was that, even while I was in high school, I had been drawn to the reflection on the sufferings, passion, and death of our Lord. Now in considering an active community, I thought that I would see if I would be accepted in an order with devotion to the Passion of Christ. The religious order that I had in mind would present a problem to my mother. She had gone to a great deal of trouble to see to it that I would not be educated by a religious community from that order. When I was graduating from the eighth grade, my mother actually went to the bishop, Bishop Rehring, auxiliary bishop of Cincinnati, and obtained his permission for me to attend a high school run by the Sisters of Charity of Mt. St. Joseph. This required special permission because the high school to which girls from our parish were assigned was taught by the nuns that I was now choosing to apply to for admittance to their community.

Now, as far as I know, my mother had nothing against my chosen community, but her reasons had to do with her past. You see, she had been a novice in the Sisters of Charity. My mother was a very intelligent person (as can be verified by every one of her grade report cards). I still have them, and in her eight years, she never received a grade lower than 90. However, she thought that God was angry with her because, as a novice, she had left the community of the sisters.

While there may have been a number of reasons why she left the order, the one that she gave me was what you might call a sensible decision. You see, while she was intelligent, she only had a grade school education. Therefore, as a novice, she was being trained in domestic work, i.e., cooking and cleaning. She had as part of her assignment to complete the final cleaning of the day for the kitchen, which was a rather large area for the motherhouse community. As a result, she was usually late for community prayers. The novice mistress informed her that for every minute that she was late for community prayers, she would have to spend that amount of time added to her time in purgatory. So, my sensible mother said to herself,

"I did not enter a religious community to add time to my purgatory." Her novice mistress told her that she did not have a vocation. The priest, who was her confessor, told her that the novice mistress had no right to tell her that. Nevertheless, my mother, then Sister Alma Louise, returned home. And for the remainder of her life feared death, because she felt that everything that was bad that happened to her was because God was punishing her.

So, it was her ambition to appease the anger of God by giving him a priest—my brother Jack (who did not comply with her conviction that he was supposed to be a priest) and a nun—a Sister of Charity—myself.

Even when I decided to enter a religious life, I felt that I should not be a Sister of Charity. I knew that I would not be able to make my reasons clear to my mother, so I didn't try. My reasoning went like this: the Sisters of Charity at my high school thought well of me. I had a great fear of pride, and so I didn't want to enter a community where, because I was esteemed, I would become proud. Of course, I had no way of knowing what being held in low regard was going to feel like. That knowledge was yet to come.

THE ACTIVE COMMUNITY

To my mother's chagrin, I was accepted by the community that I had chosen. The community needed an indult from Rome to receive a person who had been in another community, so I was received as a postulant, a person who was asking to be received into a religious community. The indult was eventually received, and I entered the novitiate with the group of postulants that I had been with. After one year of novitiate, I was told that, since I had already completed another novitiate in the cloister, I would be professed and sent out on mission. The rest of the group would complete the customary second year of novitiate. I don't know how it is done now, but at that time, newly professed nuns received the notice of their assignments (their obedience) in an envelope at their place at the dinner table.

Now, as a postulant, I had expressed an interest in being a nurse. I was encouraged in that interest by being tutored in a science class that I would need for entering nursing school. When I opened my "obedience," I was shocked to find that I was assigned to teach a sixth-grade class at Falls Church, Virginia. I had never considered teaching (which was rather stupid, as I was entering a teaching community). I had no training in teaching—not one ounce of training in how to teach and had the unpleasant memory of how poorly I handled a few preschool youngsters. I went into disbelief and for several months felt numb, as if I was going through the motions of something that I did not grasp. I could not understand what was happening.

Well, if anyone thinks that holy obedience means that if your superior tells you to do something, God will enable you to do it. Let me tell you that is not always true. It is outstandingly obvious that there was absolutely no danger of me committing a sin of pride while at Falls Church, Virginia, at least in the teaching area. (I had crumb of smugness that occurred later on.)

The current sixth grade teacher wanted nothing to do with my initiation into teaching. So, I was assigned to teach fifth grade. I had fifty-four active energetic youngsters to teach in an unfinished classroom that had no blackboards. The classroom was crowded. This was in the era of post war baby boomers. Every Catholic School had a waiting list of applicants who could not be accepted because of overcrowding. Some of the nuns tried to help me become a disciplinarian by having me stand in front of a mirror, learning to have a stern expression on my face. While I don't think I quite mastered that while at Falls Church, I did later in my teaching career when I could quell eighth grade boys by becoming silent and simply looking at them. It is quite a weapon, that look.

However, the Falls Church experience wasn't all bad. I previously mentioned my brief but enjoyable foray into smugness. Well, our good generous Irish pastor at Falls Church treated the nuns to a fishing trip on the Potomac River. Now, I might not have been able to control 54 fifth graders, but I could bait my own hook and needed no assistance in taking a captured fish off the hook, thank you very much. And I caught the expression of admiration and, I suspect a bit of gratitude, on the face of the young assistant priest who had been bidden by the pastor to be with us that day. I wasn't one of those crying, "Oh, Father...," now was I? Nope, not me.

That was on a Saturday. On Sundays, we had mass in our chapel but always attended another mass in the parish church. Well, another young sister and myself decided, what with our sunburned faces (that was the only parts of our bodies that had been exposed to the sun, our habits and veils covered all the rest of us), that it would be too embarrassing to be seen. So, we decided to stay in the convent rather than to be subjected to the stares and comments of the parishioners. The good pastor would have none of that. He sent for us to come to church. So, we were forced to face the embarrassment of an amused congregation as we tried to slip into our pews.

Another treat while I was at Falls Church was a trip to New York. The good pastor paid for the whole household of us to go to New York to see off sisters of our community who were sailing to South America to establish a mission there, joining brothers and priests. None of us had ever been to New York, so we were a bunch of gawky sightseers. It was Christmastime, and the animated windows in the department stores delighted us. We also reveled in being able to ride the elevator to the top of the Empire State Building without charge. That was a permanent stipulation of Al Smith, former mayor of New York City, that all nuns were to be allowed to ride to the top without charge.

Despite these interesting diversions, I was not happy with the Falls Church experience, and when speaking to the Mother General of the community during retreat, as was customary, I advised her that I did not intend to make final vows next year.

I was not sent back to Falls Church, but when "obediences" came out, I was assigned to a parish in a suburb of Cincinnati. There I was excited to be part of an integrating community.

Historically, what had happened was that Cincinnati City officials (I presume with the voters' approval) had arranged for the demolishing of inner city slums. Realtors had been given the opportunity to go into the suburbs, spreading the rumor that a black family would be moving into the neighborhood. Were the current residents interested in selling their homes? Well, many did just that. However, there was a wonderful group of truly Christian Catholics who embraced the opportunity to be part of an integrating community. Their children were delightful to teach, and the "black" children were sweet and very cooperative. In addition, I found out that I had caught onto the knack of teaching. The pastor was pleased with me and had even written to the motherhouse, requesting my return the next year.

I changed my mind and resolved to make final vows after all.

But, of course, there was a wrinkle in all of this. One day, the sister from the motherhouse who was in charge of assignments came to visit us. She spoke to me privately with obvious anger and resentment. She showed me a letter that she had received from the diocesan priest responsible for overseeing all diocesan schools. The monsignor upbraided her in the letter for putting me into teaching while having absolutely no credentials. I remember that he said in the letter that no nun without any college education should be put into teaching. I could not, at that time, figure out why this nun from the motherhouse was mad at me. It was quite a few years later before I came to the conclusion that she must have thought that I had gone to the monsignor or had gotten someone else to do so on my behalf. Neither of which even entered my mind.

So, off I went, after one year in Cincinnati, to Fort Wayne, Indiana. Here I taught a double grade fifth and sixth, which was a good preparatory experience. Shortly after my arrival in Fort Wayne, the superior of the nuns, who was also the principal of the school and a rather formidable person in physical build as well as personality, expressed some chagrin, because she had been informed by the nun in charge of education at the motherhouse that another nun and myself would be attending evening college. The superior was very adverse to any of her nuns going to school while also teaching; she felt that it was just too much. But she had been given no input in the decision, which appeared to have already finalized with completed applications from the motherhouse.

But she did not surrender easily. The house did not have a car, so the superior told me that I would have to recruit volunteer drivers from the list of parents of children enrolled in our school.

I was given a caveat: each parent was to serve only once, either in driving to the college or in picking us up from the college to bring us home.

I took the parent list with telephone numbers and a calendar and proceeded to make calls.

When I took the completed calendar to the superior, she was angry. I suspected that she did not foresee my success. So I asked her if she wanted me to return and cancel my request. No, she could not do that. So my companion and I began to attend night classes.

During that year, I was confined to bed on three occasions, twice for episodes of tonsillitis and once for a siege of Asiatic flu. The latter was described as, "First, you're afraid that you're going to die and then you're afraid that you won't." It was fortunate for me that the fear of contagion kept visitors away, because having a heavy reading requirement for one of the courses, I had a lot of time in which I could read until the handle of the door to my room moved. Then I quickly slid the book under the covers. My companion and I were pleased to have done well.

However, three health-related episodes gave the superior the ability to have the motherhouse schedule a tonsillectomy and an assignment to the warmer climate of California. The travel westward would have to proceed soon after my surgery. I could not talk and was on a soft, well liquid diet. Therefore, we—myself and several other nuns assigned to western missions—would have to go by train (not the usual lengthy car trip). This was a really enjoyable and genuinely educational experience. As we wended through towns, tunnels, and hills, our porters regaled us with stories about other experiences they had in their work. There was the experience with a "nun" who did not act like a typical nun. You see, there was an advantage to being a clergyman or religious woman. Such qualified persons rode the trains on "clergy" rates. So the person in question, according to the porter, while being appropriately garbed in religious clothes did not act quite right. You see, the porter explained that she was always found to be praying when he checked to make sure that everything was all right. He said that he knew that just wasn't right.

Real sisters, he said, pray awhile, read awhile, sleep awhile. They never pray all the time. So he alerted the authorities, and they confronted and took the feigned "sister" into custody.

I had now been teaching in four years in states from Virginia to California. My new assignment was in an academy, which offered both day classes for grades one through eight and high school, as well as boarding for girls in those classes. A new experience awaited me. I would be teaching in a four-room school and supervising the grade school boarders. Of course, all classes in the four-room school was a double class. I would be teaching grades seven and eight with each teaching day followed by the supervision of twenty-seven little girls. My bedroom was between two dormitories, the little girls and the big girls (those in high school). There were two sliding panels, one on each side wall, through which I could observe the boarders, checking for any untoward behavior. The "little" girls were no major problem, except for a bout of homesickness that required some comforting. I discovered that "big" girls sometimes slipped out of the building stuffing something in the locked door to keep it open and went away to an evening of fun in the nearest town. Well, I informed the superior, who eliminated that activity.

My care of the younger boarders required that when an event was taking place for the academy high school, I needed to take the lot of younger boarders for a hike into the hills. But before we set out, we needed to call the rancher who owned the property through which we traveled, asking him to please pen up the bull, as we would be traveling through.

These outings were pleasant enough, except for the day when I asked what was the unfamiliar noise that I heard. They responded with no sign of concern, "Oh, it's just the rattlesnakes." I was not about to show any concern, but I was uncomfortable until it was time for us to depart for our return to the academy.

After the first year at the academy, I traveled back to the motherhouse with a carful of nuns returning for retreat or education, both of which were on my schedule. In regard to education, a group of us participated in the very first workshops offered at the university. That meant taking a course that lasted for solid morning and afternoon classes. As I remember, they lasted for two or three weeks. Two of us made a delightful discovery in which we prudently shared *with no one*.

At Brother Paul's Ice Cream Shop, nuns did not pay for ice cream cones. Our lunch every day consisted in a sandwich from a suitcase packed each morning and then the surreptitiously indulgent ice cream cones.

Returning to California that summer was quite an experience. Someone of "the powers that be" decided that we were too few to travel in two cars. Therefore, we were all to share one car.

That meant that three nuns were put in the back seat of the car, and then luggage was packed around their legs. And there was another wrinkle. Since the original plan was to have two cars, there were now two nuns who claimed that each had been given the "obedience" to be in charge of the trip. To make matters even more interesting, one of the nuns "in charge" had written on her obedience that we were allowed to leave the designated route in order to visit Yosemite National Park. The second "nun in charge" vehemently disagreed with this, stating that the other "nun in charge" had deceived the Mother General in getting this unusual and generous permission. Nevertheless, off to Yosemite we went.

It was evening when we arrived, and the only housing available was in a sort of camping style building occupied (as far as I can remember) by a number of women. There was, of course, not much privacy. So "nun in charge" two was very vehement in her disapproval, which hit an all-time high when a few of us went out in the dark to view the ceremony (one no longer performed) of sending a ball of fire down the face of a mountain.

It was a thrilling sight, well worth the scolding we got from "nun in charge" two.

However, we all arrived safely, and I rather imagine that Mother General read the aggrieved letter from "nun in charge" two and filed it in "the round grey receptacle."

My second year at the academy was made more interesting because the nun who had been principal of the grade school was transferred, and I was the new principal. Not that it meant much, there was very little principal activity to be done in a four-room school.

It did continue to be very gratifying. I really enjoyed the activity-filled days, and I was disappointed when I was advised that it was too expensive to send me back and forth each summer, and there was a problem with the university accepting off campus credits. Now, I suspect that was probably not the complete story, because I continued to attend school "off campus" later on.

So, here I was with a new "obedience" to Wapakoneta, Ohio. At that time, it seemed to be a typical rural community. I am confident, due to the influence of Neil Armstrong, there is now a different atmosphere, a sophistication not present in the two years that I taught there. When I was there, there was a strong adherence to long held values that gave the entire environment and its citizens a sense of security.

My next assignment was a gift from God. This assignment took me to the town in which I grew up. This was providential because in May of that year, my mother was diagnosed with colon cancer, had surgery followed by x-ray treatments. The later had left her with blackened skin and also so very weak that she was bedridden. I obtained permission to care for my mother rather than to attend school that summer. In the following year, I was allowed, after a day of teaching, to walk the several blocks to my parent's home to care for my mother. The doctor had taught me how to give morphine shots and to give the prescribed tablets to my mother. So

I relieved my sister-in-law who had been with my mother since my father had left for work in the morning. I cared for mother and fixed dinner for the three of us, cleaned up, and my father drove me back to the convent. There I did my daily task of sweeping the chapel floor, prepared the next day's lessons, said my prayers, went to bed, and begin the routine again the following day.

Mother died on Easter Tuesday, April 12, 1966. I had called the superior of the convent on the previous day and received reluctant permission to stay overnight as my mother had slipped into a coma, and I was told by the doctor that she was dying. My sister-in-law was with me. As I stood beside my mother's bed, my sister-in-law drew me away, telling me to rest. I was awakened by a change in my mother's breathing and went to her side to pray for her as her life slipped away. I was thankful that she was not conscious when she experienced the moment that she feared for so many years. I was confident that she then realized that her fears were unwarranted as she met her loving Lord.

I was concerned for my father who had several attacks of angina in the following months. I asked the Mother General if I could remain at my present assignment so I could be a support to my father. She replied that I was not to stay; I was to get another assignment. And so, I was given my seventh assignment in eleven years.

MY TRUTH

What I am about to tell you is so important that I am going to begin it with a prayer—a favorite of mine from St. Thomas Aquinas:

Incomprehensible Creator, the true fountain of life and only author of all knowledge, vouchsafe to remove from us all darkness of sin and ignorance. Thou who makes eloquent the tongues that want utterance, give us a diligent and obedient spirit, quickness of apprehension, the capacity of retaining and the powerful assistance of Thy holy grace that what we hear (or read) may apply to Thy honor and glory and the welfare of our immortal souls.

My reason for writing this is not that I hope to be believed in. I no longer consider that to be of any importance. My purpose is simply to relate the truth because truth, our truth, is a beautiful, open manifestation of what the Divine Artisan works with in making us, each one of us, our unique truth, a new creation.

This part of my narrative begins with my arrival at my next assignment. Here, a somewhat older nun began to pay a lot of attention to me. She befriended me with interest and kindness. I confess that a weakness I have in my personality is that I deeply desire to be treated with kindness. I also am naïve, and unless the good God gives me his strength, I would rather go along with another than question and criticize someone. (Except if the person is in a teaching position. Then I will attack any erroneous statements with vehemence.)

I allowed this woman to seduce me sexually. I did not permit her to touch me in an impure and sinful way, but I acquiesced to her wishes. Horrified at what was happening, I struggled to figure out how I would get out of this situation. (Unfortunately, it never occurred to me to just tell her that I was no longer going to do what she was asking. I really was a doofus.) I remembered words of counsel given to me by my spiritual director when I was in high school.

He had advised me, "Always be open with your confessor and your superior."

So, I went to confession, acknowledging what was happening. His words were, "You deserve better than that." Then silence. Finally, he gave me my penance and absolution.

Since I had received no help there, I asked to go to the motherhouse to speak to the Mother General. Instead, she came to our convent. I met with her privately and told her what was happening. She shared that information with the superior of the house who told all the sisters what I had said. The accused nun denied any responsibility and said that I was the perpetrator.

And everyone believed her. The statement that she gave (and continued to give over the years) with conviction is, "I never touched her. She touched me." That, of course, was not the whole truth. I would not allow her to touch me. However, I presume she could pass a lie detector test with that statement. Consequently, to this day, an entire community of nuns, an entire community of priests, many priests in an entire diocese, many women in a parish and beyond look at me as a person to be wary of, lest I attempt to seduce them. It has been a heart-piercing experience when a woman shrinks from me, when a priest belittles me.

Of course, when the meeting of the nuns of the convent and the outcome of that meeting was relayed to me, I knew that I would have to leave the community, because the story would spread like wildfire.

This was before the great exodus when many religious and priests left their religious lives. So this was a major disgrace. I was told how I was to leave; slip out surreptitiously in the early hours before anyone was up for the day. To this day, I can see it all emblazoned in my memory.

The difficult part of all this was: first, my weakness in allowing all of this to happen; second, my desire had been to be truthful with my confessor and my superior. And then, about forty years later, the loss of anyone's belief in me. This, by persons whom I had loved and whose lack of belief in me, was truly painful. I was never asked about this and another false accusation, one that I am ethically and legally obliged, by laws of confidentiality, to not reveal. I also suffered from what I supposed to be satanically inspired thoughts questioning "why don't people think about rash judgment," and "why does God, who knows how I strove to be truthful, allow all of this pain?" On top of all that, I was told by my confessor that the people who were spreading calumny about me were doing evil. While struggling within myself to believe that it was all in order that God could make of me "a new creation," I also was trying to avoid persons who were being led into evil. Spiritually, I felt like I was on a roller coaster; one day I would be happy to be allowed to share in the passion of Christ who was lied about by the high priests and condemned to death, and the next day feeling sorry for myself and crying within, "Stop the world, I want to get off."

Perhaps, because God is pleased with this writing, here in the midst of telling my story, I have experienced an inner change in my spiritual life. I know that God was good. He never took his eyes off of me, nor his ears from hearing me. He kept the Holy Spirit's inspiration within me, keeping within me prayer and the sacraments, leading me deeply into the mystery of the holy sacrifice of the mass. And one day, I woke up with an inner happiness that gently suffused my whole being. The pain became more bearable.

Fortunately, there were persons who helped me to get my act together as I entered into this new phase of my life, no longer a religious.

My brother received me into his home; my sister-in-law got me some clothes (this was in the era of habits for nuns), I set about borrowing money from a church credit union, because I still had not earned my bachelor's degree in education. I enrolled for my final semester. Upon graduation, I set out to find a job. It was fall, very few openings in teaching were available. I was directed to one school, but the position had been filled. I was told about an opening at another school. At first, I was told that the opening was for a fourth grade. I declined this position, because most of my experience had been at the level of the seventh and eighth grades. A few days later, the principal called me and told me that there was now an opening for a seventh-grade teacher.

I proceeded to spend the next thirteen successful years teaching in that school. The first principal was an admirable woman who led her teachers well and blended that leadership with support of initiatives in education. She was also amazingly tolerant of what could have been labeled as poor supervision. Another teacher and myself decided, with the principal's permission, to take both of our classes to an area near the school, which was in an unfinished housing development and which had a lake in it. I was teaching language arts to both classes while the other was teaching science. We had established learning objectives for the "field trip."

We even had a camera with us to record our accomplishments. Unfortunately, the camera captured one rascal of a boy frolicking in the lake. I don't know who was the most nervous as we returned to the school building, the teachers or the guilty boy. The principal was a strong disciplinarian. Even the unruliest lad held her in awe. However, no one got into trouble over this escapade. This was an example of her wisdom and understanding. Her follower as principal was of the old school and not as supportive in any lesson plans that appeared to be innovations.

The next principal was a rather interesting person who was more away from her office and the school than in it. She enjoyed interacting socially with the parents of the school students.

It is to be noted that the woman who had seduced me and accused me of being the perpetrator of seduction had also left religious life. In fact, she did so not too long after I had left. As I think back on what ensued, I am dumbfounded that I never questioned about her lying about me to everyone. I held no grudge against her. There was no further attempt at seduction, however. Why did I just act as if nothing had happened, and why had she left the convent? I began to realize that something was very much amiss when I began making plans to leave the city. Her reaction was extremely emotional. I realize now that she suffered from what appeared to be a deep-seated personality disorder. My moving away was a blow to her. And, I presume, contributes to her ongoing protestations of my guilt in what she had, in fact, perpetrated.

A NEW PATH

At this point, after thirteen years teaching in this school and a total of twenty-five years of teaching, somehow my joy in teaching was slipping away like the air leaking from a balloon. I decided to leave teaching. In retrospect, perhaps I was influenced by the disappointment that I had experienced in the previous school year. I had been given authorization from the principal to teach algebra to the top mathematics students. My expectation was that they would then be placed in an advanced class in high school. They were not. They were placed in a class with algebra books that I would give to students with limited ability. I felt very bad, because I had worked these youngsters hard. I wanted them to see how far they could go with their God-given talent and hard work. But my attempt was a failure. All it gave them was an easy freshmen class in algebra. I suppose that I was depressed by this failure. I also felt badly by the experience of having high school students dropping in after school to visit and regaling me with tales of their antics. I grieved that these were children whom I had prepared for the reception of the sacrament of confirmation were now bragging about their unholy experiences.

While I can now analyze contributions to my feelings of depression, at the time I attributed my decision to leave teaching as simply wanting something else. I would definitely not advise this to anyone—that is, leaving one profession when you have absolutely no sense of further direction. It is definitely not a smart move, but that was just what I did.

I wanted to go to school to learn spirituality. Today, I would be able to choose from quite a number of schools that offer just that. But "back in the day," if there were any, I could not find them. I was advised by a person who was renowned as being a very holy person to make a thirty-day retreat at a Jesuit retreat house, and so I did. My thirty days were marked by a case of poison ivy and a bout with the flu. In engaging in the discernment process, I ended with "stay here and get direction." I thought that meant spiritual direction. So, I signed up for spiritual direction. I think that I must have been a training activity for a young Jesuit.

Meanwhile, I rented a house in the Winton Place area of Cincinnati where the New Jerusalem Community, a charismatic community, was based. I had been and continued to be intrigued by Jungian analytical psychology. In fact, I had convened a coterie of three or four women and myself, which met to study and discuss Jungian topics provided by a Jungian learning center. In addition, a friend referred me to a psychologist who, while not trained in Zurich, was Jungian in bent. So, I began therapy. Well, he was not only somewhat Jungian, but also had been trained in Fritz Pearl Gestalt psychology.

I found therapy to be very spiritual, so I decided that would be my next career. My therapist stated that I would need to get my doctorate and that I needed to get it in a PsyD program (doctorate in psychology as differing from a PhD program, which places an emphasis on research; whereas a PsyD program has a greater emphasis on getting practical supervised experience). At least, that was the difference at that time.

My first need was to get credits in a number of psychology courses (my bachelor and my master's degrees were both in education). I enrolled in Xavier University for some of these courses and the University of Cincinnati for others. I also signed up for a review course in psychology, the Kaplan Course. This despite the research that seemed to give evidence that it was not a substantial help in the Graduate Record Exams (GRE). My results proved the research to be unsubstantiated, which just shows that one cannot always believe research. While in the midst of all this, I took the GRE exams. I took the general exam first. I was so nervous that, in getting ready to go for the test, I accidently sprayed my hair with bathroom cleaner instead of hair spray. So, despite a hasty attempt to towel it off, I went to the exam smelling like a clean bathroom.

Because of, I presume, rotating GRE psychology exams, I went to Indiana for this exam. I was quite peaceful now. I thought that if I was intended to pass this, I would. If not, I could always settle for getting a master's degree.

As I took the test, I remembered that one was advised not to guess at answers. But since I was finished before time was up, I went back over items that I had skipped and guessed. It must have been an okay ploy, because I did well on that test.

Then I set about sending out applications to seven PsyD programs. I was accepted at two and chose the school located in Ohio because my father, now in a nursing home, was in Ohio, and I would be close enough to visit him. On Easter Sunday, I visited him and told him that I had been accepted in the school in Ohio. On Easter Tuesday, he died of a massive heart attack.

I auctioned off my furniture and other belongings and headed for my new campus. The program for the PsyD program was lockstep with three years of classes accompanied with practicum sites and one year of pre-doctoral internship. The assignments to these training sites required applications and being accepted by an approved internship practice site. In applying for an internship, I concentrated on those offered by Veteran Administrations, because I was favorably impressed by the supervision that I had received from the supervisors at the VA. I was not accepted at any of the sites to which I had applied. Sticking to my resolve of doing my internship at a VA, I asked for help from the psychology department head at the VA. I then found a VA that would accept me. It was in a consortium in South Dakota. The work sites were in the VA and in two community mental health clinics. The training offered me was excellent. I had for my clients Native Americans, Vietnam veterans, typical adults and teenagers, the whole range of diagnoses, and served as a testifying psychologist in a custody court case. In addition, I took a trip through Wyoming during a work break.

In retrospect, I suppose that I must have presented a bit of a challenge to the analytically inclined professors and deans of the university. When I presented myself for an education to be awarded with a doctorate in psychology, a woman in her late forties who showed herself to be intelligent, not unattractive, nothing unappealing in her demeanor, one would ask why she is not married. If she is a homosexual, we have to help her come out of "the closet." There is something amiss with her, and we have to identify it before she leaves the university.

In addition to what I suspect were their concerns, I had revealed a trait that aroused deep concern. I was independent. I had successfully worked with a difficult client while my supervisor at the practicum site was not aware of what I had accomplished. I had faithfully kept notes on each session with the client in the client's file. However, my supervisor never checked my files (he was not required to do so) and never questioned me about what I was doing in therapy. He preferred telling me what he was doing. While I resolved that, if he should show an interest in what I was doing, I would tell him about what I was doing with all the clients assigned to me. I acknowledge that I was relieved that he never veered from elaborating about himself. Because I was very glad that I could continue to help the client whose need was very great.

You see, the fact was that I used hypnotherapy in my successful treatment. I had availed myself of an opportunity to get training in hypnotherapy while I was in the VA practicum site.

One of my supervisors there had remarked that he thought I would do well in hypnotherapy because of the quality of my voice. So, I had permission from the head of the psychology department to attend a training workshop in hypnotherapy.

In working with the client in question, it had required several weeks of telephone therapy before he consented to come into the clinic. In an early interview, he spontaneously went into a trance as I was helping him to relax. I checked on a hypnotic suggestion that I had given him verifying his quality as a subject. I kept tapes of each session in addition to the written records in his file.

Evidently, the clinic supervisor became aware of the successful outcome of the therapy through the client's wife who, of course, must have observed her husband's dramatic change for the better. I had no intention of announcing the happy outcome. I had been told, before the practicum began, that I was going to be supervised in hypnotherapy by the clinic supervisor, but another student was assigned to this supervisor.

Now all evidence of my success had to be destroyed. It had never occurred to me, but the fact that I had been acting without supervision (through no fault of my own) would put the school in a very grave situation, if it came to light.

The first thing that needed to happen was that I needed to be chastised before a "court" of inquiry. It was a sort "you'd better not tell anyone about this or there will be serious reprisals." Although I had already received an "A" in this semester's supervision, I now was given a letter of correction and disapproval.

I took my tapes, the ones from my therapy sessions with the client in question, to one of the deans who reviewed them and acknowledged that I had done good work. Then he told me to destroy the tapes. I was just happy that the therapy had been successful in returning the client to his former status of good mental health.

However, you see how nervous I made the deans feel about me. I think that they had a very clear preference for me to remain on campus for my pre-doctoral internship. But I succeeded in being accepted into the internship in South Dakota.

There remained an uncertainty about my sexual orientation. And, to be honest, there lurked in my unconscious an uncertainty because of the interaction I had been drawn into with the older nun. I had attempted to address this while I was a client in psychotherapy, but the therapist minimized my concern, and the topic was not explored.

Part of me thinks that the situation that I am about to describe came from the dean's uncertainty about my sexual orientation. Perhaps, "if she's in the closet, we have to help her out of it before she can be trusted as a therapist."

But the source of what transpired could be unrelated to any concern of theirs. So, with a deep breath, I will share what happened and thereby show another example of my total unworthiness for the lovingkindness of the heart of my God. I ask our God that he be strongly present in this revealing of my truth and confirm in me pure motives in the manifestation of my weakness and sinfulness.

Here is the story. In one of the two mental health clinic sites, there was a therapist, Pete. He invited me to go out with him. At first, I refused. He was persistent but not obnoxiously so. I began to agree. I succumbed to his sexual advances, perhaps at a deep need to have my heterosexuality confirmed. However, he evidently accomplished whatever he intended to prove, because he then dropped me. I found out later that he had done the same thing with a previous intern.

Later, I thought that I would do for myself what any therapist would do for a client who needed a sense of certainty regarding her sexuality. I began to explore my earliest relationship with the opposite sex.

First, there was "Tody." We were either prekindergarten or kindergarten age. We were at a party, I guess a birthday party, and Tody and I hit it off and played together at the birthday games all afternoon. I remember one of the mothers remarking about our being together. An "aren't they cute together?"

This was said to my mother—the mother who had decided that I was to become a nun. I don't remember Tody visiting us again.

Then in grade school, I had a couple of crushes on boys. There was Paul, who was not only good-looking, he was smart. He sent me a valentine one Valentine's Day.

He probably sent every girl a valentine. But I kept his valentine for a long time and even remember the words on it "U R O K." Then, in the eighth grade, there came on the scene the almost movie star-like boy. He had been at a military school while his parents were away. But now they moved into the neighborhood, and their son was in our eighth grade. He even had a uniform! Of course, I was just one of the awestruck following that he had. My mother noticed and informed me that we were related to his family.

In writing this, I recall that this was the mother who intended that I be a nun. It was also the mother who overfed us on cakes, pie, and ice cream, ending in two very overweight children.

Was this a ploy to keep us from being attractive?

We only had all girl and all boy high schools in parochial schools in those days. I do recall, quite vividly, being on a picnic when a soldier in uniform was introduced to our family. I stood up straight and tried to smooth down my hair. His girlfriend was with him, and she punched his side while laughing at me. But, oh my, he was a thrilling sight to see.

Of course, all the teachers were nuns, but I simply admired and was grateful to the good ones who really taught well. I never had a crush on any female who came into my life. I had friends, but the ones I had in high school were only friends because I helped them with their homework.

Later in life, to some extent, I knew what I was letting myself in for when I asked another woman if she wanted to move in with me. But the reason was not because I wanted companionship of any kind. I loved and still love solitude. I offered my home because I knew her limited ability to live alone. I could not in conscious, knowing what could happen, knowing how great her risk was, fail to offer her a home. And I fully realized that I was quite likely to be labeled a homosexual. However, I had no idea that I would be labeled a homosexual predator.

As is evident, there is much that show my weakness, my sinfulness and therefore bear witness to the tremendous love of our God, not just for me but for all weak, sinful, needy persons. He really meant it when he said, "I came for sinners."

In regard to my internship in South Dakota, I received very favorable reports and graduated. I was now a doctor of psychology.

After graduation, I asked the pastor of the parish that I had attended while living in Winton Place in Cincinnati, if, after the Sunday Liturgy, I could consecrate my work as a psychologist to God. He agreed, and I stood before the congregation and consecrated my work as a psychologist to God. I have frequently been keenly aware of the presence and power of the Holy Spirit in my work.

And so, having graduated and again looking for a job, I contacted a friend whose daughter I had taught, asking for his help in finding a job. I knew that he had contacts in the mental profession. He did direct me to a mental health clinic where I was hired. The environment was somewhat unpleasant, and I had difficulty in interacting with the supervisor. When I saw an ad from a facility in Massachusetts, I put in an application, was called for an interview, and was hired. I had read books published by this organization when I was in high school and was hopeful of being allied with a spiritual path of psychology.

In my time of working there, I was asked to give a talk on the Jungian psychology of the shadow. I did so and was then sent to St. Louis to give the presentation to a national conference.

This presentation was audio taped. Therein unfolded my series of presentations on Jungian psychology—audiotaped by what was then called Alba House Press.

But the facility at which I worked went under financially, and I was again job hunting. I left Massachusetts and decided on Cleveland, because there were several sites there that were advertising for a psychologist (I had been licensed in Ohio by now). I was not immediately successful in getting a job. But I did eventually succeed in being hired as a psychology supervisor in a home for children who were placed there by the court as a place for temporary residence and psychological care. In the meantime, I was repeatedly called by one of the examiners from the Ohio licensing oral exam, offering me a position in the Ohio Department of Rehabilitation and Correction, the state prison system.

I finally agreed to an interview for the job, not only because of the higher salary that was offered but also because of the excellent benefits. I did not get the first job for which applied, but a second one was quickly offered, and I was on board.

It was a difficult but really good job. It turned out to be much more rewarding than I would ever have suspected. I even had the opportunity to develop a Jungian-based sex offender program.

Then after thirteen years working as a psychology supervisor in a state prison, I retired at the age of seventy-one.

Now, a whole new life began. We are told not to wait for retirement to pursue a deeper spiritual life. But sometimes, it just works out that way. For me, after retiring, I had a repeating inner insistence that I should be assisting at mass daily. But I countered, "I have enrolled in a health center, and I work out every morning. I cannot do both." Well, I began to feel progressively weaker, and my numbers for weight lifting dropped dramatically. I went to the doctor in the first week of January and was subsequently sent to a succession of specialists and finally, in May, had a thyroidectomy. There were several tumors in my thyroid gland, but none were cancerous.

Then I began a regime beginning with daily mass, spiritual reading, and the books seemed to come to my hands. Each morning, I got to church as soon as it was opened and spent time before mass reading and meditating on Benedict XVI's book *The Spirit of the Liturgy*. Over and over, I read and meditated. Then one day, as I genuflected, I heard the words, "In the Liturgy, you enter the life of God." Wow, what an experience! But I thought I had better check it out.

It turned out to be years of asking priests about these words as well as searching the catechism and other books, but never finding these words. I found words that I could interpolate, but not the same words. Finally, I read, *The Way*, the documentation of the movement toward unity between the Lutheran Evangelical Church and the Roman Catholic Church. Here I found three areas that affirmed the words that I had heard. And I found one priest who quite definitely affirmed the validity of the words.

In addition, there were experiences that contributed to my being tremendously drawn into the mystery of the Liturgy of the mass. As events unfolded, I suspected that, by gifting me in this way, our Lord held me in the church, because there were very difficult times ahead of me.

After over forty years of no mention of what caused me to leave religious life, I began to be harassed and to experience assaults of calumny and the spreading of lies by persons who are respected and believed in. Friends whom I dearly loved were no longer my friends, and persons to whom I had confided now routinely betrayed my confidence.

The woman who, as a nun, had seduced me continued to spread lies about me. She was believed by nuns and priests, who warned other priests. Women of my parish were warned about me. This was augmented by clients of a facility at which I had worked, who had, evidently spied on a therapy session and believed that they had seen inappropriate behavior. As indicated above, as a psychologist, I am bound by the ethics of the profession, federal law, and state law, all of which forbid me to divulge anything about a client or anything about a client's therapy. I cannot divulge that a person is or was a client.

In all of this, there were the words of God the Father to St. Catherine of Siena:

There is another thing you must do to attain this union and purity: You must never pass judgment in human terms on anything you see or hear from anyone at all, whether it concerns you or someone else. You must consider only my will for them and you.

And if you should see something that is clearly a sin or fault, snatch the rose from that thorn. In other words, offer these things to me in holy compassion. As for any assault against yourself, consider that my will permits it to prove virtue in you and in my other servants. Assume that the offender does such a thing as an instrument commissioned by me. For often such a person's intention is good; there is no one who can judge the hidden heart.

As I indicated above, I struggled with these words for years. What helps me now to embrace these words is the deepening of the realization of what it means to be made a new creation. What happened to me occurred because of my weakness. One of my favorite words from Sacred Scripture are these lines from Sirach (11:12):

Another goes his way, a weakling and a failure, with little strength and great misery. Yet the eyes of the Lord look upon him; he raises him up free of the vile dust, lifts up his head and exalts him to the amazement of the many.

If God loves me enough, if God trusts me enough to send me that which will make me a new creation, all that is asked of me is to hold in compassionate love the instruments of his infinite love, and love him and trust him in return. I have struggled to see his infinite love in all that he has done. And my greatest desire is that God may be glorified in these words that I believe that he has bidden me to write.

I am deeply, profoundly aware of my weakness. I am overwhelmingly confounded by God's goodness and merciful love toward me. It is my deepest, greatest wish that what I have written, trusting that it all has come from God, will give glory to him. I hope that it will be one small gift of beauty to him who makes of us a new creation.

As N.T. Wright has said so powerfully (*Surprised by Hope*. Grand Rapids, Michigan: Zondervan, 2010), we are each called, by whatever small and seemingly insignificant way, to contribute beauty and justice into the world. Our small contribution joins other small contributions and is a part in the whole of that new creation, which began with the resurrection of Christ from the dead and continues on until we also rise with him in the completed new creation.

I am including in this book two articles that I have written previously. The reason for including this first work, "The Threshold of Eternity," is that I wrote it in the first days of my proceeding along a pathway new to me in the journey to God. I thought that there must be others on this journey;

it could not be just for me. And I thought that it would be a comfort, an encouragement for others, walking as I did to know that they were alone among the children of God on this same journey. So I wrote this article, never before published, but which I now hope will reach out to at least some of those others walking ever nearer to eternity.

6

THE CHALICE

My friend, Judy, and I had decided that we were going to put together our jewelry and take it to a jeweler and give the proceeds to charity. However, in executing this decision, I felt uncomfortable in including a ring that, years ago, I had made from my parents' wedding rings and had included a diamond in that ring.

So, the thought came to me to purchase a chalice and to have placed on the chalice my parents' rings, the diamond, and two white gold rings that Judy and I had bought as joint affirmation to our gift of ourselves to the church. I would then send the chalice to the Passionist Nuns of St. Joseph Monastery in Whitesville, Kentucky. This was the community that I had entered at age seventeen, after I graduated from high school. I remained in this community for five years.

As indicated, they were five very difficult years in which I experienced a lot of physical pains and several hospital visits. When I returned from the last hospital visit, I suspected that I would be asked to leave the community. I resolved that I would leave if the Bishop said that I must go.

When Mother Superior came into my cell, her first words were, "The Bishop said that you must leave." She proceeded to tell me that the request for exclaustration would be submitted by the Bishop.

I could not protest the clear indication of God's will. And, I did not realize how painful this had been for me, until, sixty-four years later. I called a friend, Ann, at a religious goods store and began to tell my story, and that I wanted to buy a chalice and to have gold and the diamond placed on the chalice which I would then send to the Passionist Nuns of St, Joseph Monastery in Kentucky. As I started to tell my story, I began to sob. I realized at that moment how wrenchingly painful it had been to leave the cloister.

Ann understood and she also understood the longing I had to have something of myself at the monastery, so she sent me a catalogue. I selected a chalice and ordered it. She gave me some direction toward a jeweler who would possibly help me. The jeweler asked me about what I wanted done and why. He accepted my story with what I experienced as extraordinary kindness.

The chalice, the gold, and the diamond were entrusted to a master goldsmith who, because he believed in the sincerity of my story, produced a beautiful chalice without charging for his truly masterful work.

The entire scenario filled me with awe. It was so clearly a gift from God. In the presence of the chalice in the Monastery, I now had a presence myself in the Monastery.

Shortly thereafter, I had an awareness that my mother and my father knew, in heaven, that their wedding rings adorned the chalice. Then, in my heart, I heard my father, who had a lovely tenor voice, sing:

> *You are the Spirit of Christmas*
> *The star on the tree,*
> *The Easter Bunny to mommy and me,*
> *You are sugar and spice*
> *And everything nice,*
> *You are Daddy's little girl.*

The Chalice symbolized how our loving God had led me into the mystagog of the Holy Sacrifice of the mass, and gave a concrete understanding of how, as a member of the Mystical Body of Christ, I am present at every mass offered throughout the world.

Daddy's Little Girl

7

THE FAITH THAT WE SHARE

While these writings come heavily tinged by my Catholic background, I am very much aware that the beliefs expressed are shared by quite a few other religions. The over fifty years of dialogue between the leaders of the Apostolic Lutherans, the Methodists, and leaders in the Catholic church, show a strong confirmation of shared beliefs, convincing me that experiences that I have had in living my faith are not singular to me, or would be of little or no meaning to the faithful of other Christian churches. We share far more than we differ.

To me, the deepest meaning that I have gleaned from all that I have experienced is that Jesus Christ meant what he said when he stated, "I have come for the sinners." I don't think that there are just some kind of elite Christians called to receive personal experiences of His presence and His love. I believe that every person, with no exception, just needs to ask Him for the grace to receive His love and His revelation of Himself. Church attendance supports that request.

Personal prayer, reading scripture, and time spent in reflection all show the sincerity of that request. All of that needs to be accompanied by the faith that one's prayer will be heard and answered. So, I am confident that every word that I have shared with you has interfaith meaning.

Therefore, I offer you the words that follow.

This is not a pious platitude, I am truly unworthy and poorly qualified, (academically) to attempt to share the overwhelming beauty of what I have perceived in the amazing truths of our Faith. I feel that I should apologize for writing about these wonders, because there are many writers with auspicious credentials who have written with greater skill than I have. I apologize, but I explain that I cannot hold within me the marvels and the wonder that I have received.

First, after lengthy consideration of the propriety of sharing events touching my mind, heart, and soul, I became convinced that the events were too great to just be for me. It didn't make any sense that it would be just for one person. I believe that all of it is meant to be shared. Therefore, with great trepidation and much prayer, I begin to ask the Triune God to speak through me. I know that in Christ we have the complete revelation of the Father. So, why write this book?

Well, I hope that the many, many others who have had experiences similar to what I relate, will feel a deeper strength in the unity of the mystical body of Christ.

The first overwhelmingly memorable kind of "knocks you off your feet" event happened as I was leaving church after mass. I mentioned this event before. However, I review the experience, in order to amplify the meaning as well to show how everything all seems to fit together. As I genuflected (my knees worked better at that time), I heard the words, I mean really heard, I suppose a locution, "In the liturgy you enter the life of God," I experienced this in 2006, but I did not write down the date of the month.

So, I went home with an "oh, my gosh" feeling and searched through the Catechism, and every book in my library about the Liturgy for that statement. I found words that I could interpolate to arrive at that conclusion, but not the actual words. Finally, after years of asking priest after priest as to the veracity of these words, I found a priest, who seemed to be learned in such things, who said, "Oh, yes, that's true and it begins with the readings."

It took more years until I finally grasped the meaning of the words. I acknowledge that I am a very slow learner in the Spiritual Life.

In putting together what I have learned from spiritual reading, prayer, meditation, and reflection, here is what I have concluded that the words were intended to convey.

In the Liturgy, the Triune God; Father, Son, and Holy Spirit, are present, truly present, not some light years away. We recognize the presence of God when the reader, the lector, concludes the reading with the statement, "the Word of the Lord." And we do find in the Catechism that Our Lord is present in the words of Scripture.

#135, The Sacred Scriptures contain the Word of God and, because they are inspired they are truly the Word of God.

Now, I want to share with you how I have come to a deeper realization of how God is present in the words of Scripture. I am sharing this because of my deep conviction that the teachings that I have received are not just for me, they are meant to be shared. And, of course we know that there are no new revelations, everything has been revealed in Christ. So, none of this is new, it is the work of the Holy Spirit to make the message in Christ a little clearer.

It was with some hesitation that I signed up to be a reader for the morning masses. I wanted to be sure that I had a pure motive for offering to do this. I have a horror of becoming proud, and I recognize that, not due to myself, I have a gift in public speaking and I was afraid that this would impair the work of the Holy Spirit.

Therefore, I began to offer all that I suffered, as a prayer to the Holy Spirit in the days preceding my days of assigned reading. I asked the Holy Spirit to touch the minds and hearts and souls of all who heard the words that I read. Then, I carefully prepared, in advance, how I was to read. But, each time that I read there was always something new in my heart and words, as I read. I attributed this to the presence of the Holy Spirit each time that I read.

But, I was given an even clearer message that the God is present in His words. I had been admitted to the official list of lectors and was periodically appointed as Lector for the Saturday mass of the Vigil. One Saturday evening, I had an unusual experience. First, the ambo from which we read was on the right side of the sanctuary (from the perspective of the sanctuary).

However, as I began to read, I experienced myself as being on the left side, looking directly at members of the congregation opposite from the regular view. As I indicated, I always prepared the readings carefully. There is a book that gives direction to readers in regard to pausing, emphasizing, pace of reading, and so on. I had prepared as usual that day. As I began to read, what was coming out of my mouth in my voice was not what I had prepared. I heard the voice coming out of my mouth but I was not speaking. As I looked out at the members of the congregation, I saw awe on many faces.

After mass, a friend came up to me and thanked me for a very moving reading. I could only say, "It wasn't me, it was the Holy Spirit."

Admittedly, that was a very powerful lesson on the presence of God in the words of Scripture.

But, there's more. I am sure that many, many persons have experienced that, when they have a need for information regarding spiritual matters, somehow, the book that they need becomes available through some medium. I had been reading the book, The Spiritual Meaning of the Liturgy by Goffredo Boselli. In that book, he quotes Origen in his Commentary on Matthew these words: "It was not the visible bread that he held in his hands which God the Word called his body, but it was the Word in whose sacrament the bread was to be broken. Nor was it the visible drink that he identifies as his blood, but it was the Word in whose sacrament libation was to be poured."

It was an amazing, "Oh, I see." I began to have a deeper realization of the presence of Christ in the very words of consecration and in how Christ, present in the words, brings about the miracle of his presence in the bread and in the wine.

The path is not always as straightforward as this for me. I said before that I am a slow learner in spiritual matters. What I am now going to share with you is an example. It took me awhile before I began to understand what it meant. Or maybe it's because it seems so very unusual.

I wrote the date down this time. It was April 2, the vigil of Mercy Sunday, 2016. Mother Angelica had died on March 27 and, because I believed that this would be her first celebration of Mercy Sunday in heaven, I asked Mother Angelica to cover me with her robe of glory so that t I could assist at the liturgy covered with her robe of glory. I was the second lector for the liturgy of the Word. As I returned to my pew, and the celebrant read the gospel and began his homily, I experienced a ray of light coming from him to me. The light was blue and red. Then, at the washing of hands, I experienced the entire sanctuary filled with a light so bright that I was unable to look into the sanctuary. The light continued until the part of the liturgy where the celebrant elevates the consecrated host and proclaims, "Behold the Lamb of God. Behold Him who takes away the sins of the world. Blessed are those called to the supper of the Lamb."

But now, as I looked into the sanctuary, I saw the celebrant, the elevated Host, an altar, but not our altar, but nothing else. There was no one else in the sanctuary.

There were no walls, no ceiling.

When I told this experience to the priest who was my confessor, he said that the message was for the whole world. I asked, "what message?" His response was, "Ask the Holy Spirit." Which loosely translates as, "I haven't the foggiest."

I prayed earnestly to the Holy Spirit, wrote down the words that came to me in prayer, then had a presentation put on DVD and sent it off to EWTN (after all Mother Angelica appeared to be involved and, if the good priest was correct about a massage that should go out to the whole world, how better than through EWTN). Except, EWTN rejected my DVD. So, it took a couple of years before what I believe was the meaning to emerge. (I was not being facetious when I said that I am a slow learner in spiritual things).

I saw a connection between the words "In the Liturgy, you enter into the life of God" and the light filling the sanctuary. The light was the presence of God in the sanctuary. The Life of God, Our God, is forever self-empting. The Father gives Himself to the Son, and gives the Son to us through the Holy Spirit. The Son gives Himself to the Father in total self-emptying, becoming man through the power of the Holy Spirit, giving himself in death, even the death of the cross.

And when we give ourselves totally, to the Father in union with Christ our head we enter the self-emptying life of God.

The life of God, the essence of the Triune God is the giving of themselves, we are called in the Liturgy to enter into that life and give ourselves, in union with Christ our head, without reserve to the Triune God.

We pray to God our Father from the beginning of the mass. At the presentation of the Lamb of God, the Father presents His Son, our Redeemer, our Savior, to us through the love that flows through the Trinity.

We are called to realize this mystery, this miracle, this sharing in the life of God.

Of course, I am not a theologian, and I truly hope that I have not stated something erroneously. However, these reflections have drawn me deeper into participation in the sacrifice of the mass.

One thing that I know for sure is that my assistance at the holy sacrifice of the mass has deepened. It is strengthening to reflect that the council fathers expressed in the documents of Vatican Two a desire for us, the people in the pews, to come to a greater realization of what it is that we do when we assist at the Holy Sacrifice of the mass. In the constitution on the Sacred Liturgy part 11, The Promotion of Liturgical Instruction and Active Participation, #14, the document states: Mother Church earnestly desires that all the faithful should be led to that conscious and active participation in liturgical celebrations which is demanded by the very nature of the liturgy. Such participation by the Christian people as "a chosen race, a royal priesthood, a holy nation, a redeemed people. (1 Pet.2:9, cf2:4–5), is their right and duty by reason of their baptism.

In the restoration and promotion of the sacred liturgy this full and active participation by all the people is the aim to be considered before all else; for it is the primary and indispensable source from which the faithful are to derive the true Christian spirit; and therefore pastors of souls must zealously strive to achieve it, by means of the necessary instruction, in all their pastoral work.

In Chapter 2 of the document, The Most Sacred Mystery of The Eucharist, #47, there is expressed that the sacrifice of the cross is present in the sacrifice of the mass. That sacrifice has been referred to as "the unbloody sacrifice of Calvary."

At the Last Supper, on the night when was betrayed, our Savior instituted the Eucharistic sacrifice of His Body and Blood. He did this in order to perpetuate the sacrifice of the Cross throughout the centuries until He should come again, and so to entrust to His beloved spouse, the Church, a memorial of His death and resurrection: a sacrament of love, a sign of unity, a bond of charity, a paschal banquet in which Christ is eaten, the mind is filled with grace, and a pledge of future glory is given to us.

In this chapter, #48 details what the fathers meant by "participation." The Church, therefore, earnestly desires that Christ's faithful, when present at this mystery of faith, should not be there as strangers or silent spectators; on the contrary, through a good understanding of the rites and prayers they should take part in the sacred action conscious of what they are doing, with devotion and full collaboration. They should be instructed by God's word and be nourished at the table of the Lord's body; they should give thanks to God; by offering the immaculate Victim, not only through the hands of the priest, but also with him, they should learn also to offer themselves; through Christ the Mediator, they should be drawn day by day into more perfect union with God and with each other, so that finally God may be all in all.

The desire to worship our God and creator is recorded from the book of Genesis, where God's approval of Abel's sacrifice over Cain's illustrates what God looks for in sacrifice made to him. God gave the Israelites very explicit directions as how he wished them to worship him. Details of priestly dress and actions are prescribed.

It is no small thing that our God asks of us. So great is the worship that he asks of us that he sends his own son to become man, to suffer for us, to die for us, to become for us our perfect sacrifice, the perfect act of worship. That perfect sacrifice, that perfect worship was made once.

Because the eternal son of God entered time while remaining eternally God, his sacrifice made in time became eternal.

#1367 "The sacrifice of Christ and the sacrifice of the Eucharist are one single sacrifice:" The victim is one and the same: the same now offers through the ministry of priests, who then offered himself on the cross; only the manner of offering is different is different. "And since in this divine sacrifice which is celebrated in the mass, the same Christ who offered himself once in a bloody manner on the alter of the cross is contained and offered in an unbloody manner…this sacrifice is truly propitiatory."

We have been given by God, in the gift of the sacrifice of his son perpetuated through time, participation in a perfect act of worship. Something that I have hoped and prayed for is that every participant in the Holy Sacrifice of the mass would know, realize, truly experience the reality of their participation.

LIVING OUR BAPTISMAL SHARING IN THE PRIESTHOOD OF CHRIST

Something else that I learned and deeply longed to share with others is the realization of the gift given to us in Baptism of sharing in the priesthood of Christ The Catechism refers to this gift in several places:

#1141 The celebrating assembly is the community of the baptized who, "by regeneration and the anointing of the Holy Spirit, are consecrated to be a spiritual house and a holy priesthood, that through all the works of Christian men they may offer spiritual sacrifices." This "common priesthood" is that of Christ the sole priest, in which his members participate.

#1305 This "character" (the indelible mark of Confirmation) perfects the common priesthood of the faithful, received in Baptism.

#1546 Christ, high priest and unique mediator, has made of the Church "a kingdom, priests for his god and Father." The whole community of believers is, as such priestly... Through the sacraments of Baptism and Confirmation the faithful are "consecrated to be...a holy priesthood.

#1591 The whole church is a priestly people. Through Baptism all the faithful share in the priesthood of Christ.

Saint Peter Chrysologus appeals to us in this sermon to realize and live our participation in our "common priesthood" whereby all of our daily works can be our sacrifice, our very bodies can be sacrifice as each of us live out our priesthood. While not the consecrated priesthood of the ordained priest, yet a share in the priesthood of Christ. In living out our Baptismal priesthood, our very lives become sacrificial, to be offered in union with the sacrifice of the mass, united with the moment of Calvary continued through time. How transforming to be aware of our "common priesthood," thereby giving our mundane tasks a sacrificial value. There is yet another amazing facet to our faith, our relationship with God that astounds us. It is Almighty God's respect for the gift that He has given in our free will.

John Cardinal O'Connor gives us a soul stirring insight to this aspect of our relationship with our God. In his homily of May 3, 2019, in the EWTN televised Celebration of the mass, Father John Paul Mary, Franciscan of the Divine Word, recounted Cardinal O'Connor's words written to the sisters of the community he established, The Sisters For Life. Cardinal O'Connor recalled that during the ceremony of his ordination as a bishop at the Cathedral of St. Peter and Paul in Rome, he left the procession to walk up to Mother Theresa. They had never met. Mother Theresa looked at him and said, "Give God Permission." The Cardinal then related that he compared this to a procedure familiar to him from his 27 years of service in the military in the navy and the marines. He said that he often pondered the procedure by which a person was allowed to come on board a ship. Cardinal O'Connor explained that one of the ship's staff, of any rank from the simple sailor to the highest ranking officer, was appointed to the assignment of serving as "officer of the deck." Anyone who wanted to come aboard the ship was required to call the officer of the deck and ask. "Requesting permission to come aboard, Sir" It did not matter if the person making that request was the Secretary of the Navy or of any high position. It did not matter if the officer of the deck was a lowly sailor, until he responded, "Permission granted," the requesting person was not allowed to come on board the ship.

Cardinal O'Connor applied this procedure with all of its meaning to Mother Theresa's words, "Give God Permission." He identified giving God permission to practicing obedience.

This also seems to me to be a beautiful illustration of God's respect for the gift of free will that He has given us. In my own life, God has allowed persons to use their free will to not only accept calumny but to spread lies about me. But, He offered to me the opportunity to accept the chance to be united with Him in suffering and allow Him to beautify within my soul the reflection of God to which I was called. To make of me a new creation. Now, in all truth, I have not always docilely accepted the suffering. But, I pray that, with a new understanding of the work of God, in the future, I will Give God Permission more readily.

It is undeniably moving to ponder the God of all creation before us awaiting our response to is desire to provide us with the opportunity of growing to what we were created to be. God, of course, is all knowing, He is fully aware of our desires, our decisions, and always respects our use of our free will, even if we choose to offend Him. But, in His wisdom and power, with our permission "comes aboard" to be "on deck" with us in the transformation of the choices of others that cause us pain, to be for us a means to attain grace, if we just "Give God Permission."

It seems to me to be a matter of loving God more than we love ourselves. That was part of a prayer that I always stumbled over: I love you Jesus my love, I love you more than myself (that's where I stumbled, thinking, "I really am not sure about that; I'd like it to be true but I have too much self-love for that to be true.") Perhaps, by consciously "giving God permission" to allow deeply painful things to enter my life, I can arrive at loving God more than myself.

I also think that is a more comfortable practice than "Total abandonment to Divine Providence." The total abandonment sort of felt like jumping out of an airplane flying quite high in the sky while being nervous, questioning if the parachute would open. But, being the officer the deck and giving God permission to come on board brings a deep sigh of relief. With God on board, everything will be all right. As the British express it, "God will sort it all out." There is another thing. It probably deserves its own heading, so ...

The Will of God

There are times in our lives when we wish that we could know, for sure, what God wills.

I am not talking about not committing sin. I am referring to those nebulous times when you are deciding on a course of action to take. There have been really momentous decision makings in my life and relatively less consequential events. One really big decision was when I retired from teaching. As I mentioned, I made a thirty-day retreat and completed the decision process with a rather nebulous answer. It does bring a thought to mind, "Does God care about this or not?" At that time, the spiritual philosophy seemed to be: just figure out what you want and go with it The problem was that I knew what I wanted but couldn't get it So much for that theory.

When I finally decided on becoming a psychologist, I clearly had my goals in mind. I was deeply interested in Jungian analytical psychology. I wanted to be a therapist who worked with persons who were delving into personal growth.

That never happened. I was seldom in a position in which I could lead clients into self-knowledge. In my thirty some years as being actively involved in therapy, I am confident that I was able to help a lot of people. I am grateful to God for guiding me to wherever He wanted me to go. I am also grateful that I was able to make the series of Jungian based audio tapes, back in the day when such things existed. I am grateful that I was able to develop my skills in hypnotherapy to the extent that I could help a client achieve a remarkable recovery from a debilitating event and get his life back to normal.

But, I also wonder about times when I "put out the fleece" to discover the will of God.

"Putting out the fleece" refers to the event in the bible, book of Judges 6:40, where Gideon puts out fleece and asks God to show his will according to two different requests that Gideon makes.

The concept is, if you want to know God's will in regard to what you are to do in a particular situation, you ask God to let you know his will by fulfilling some particular action. I don't make a habit of using this kind of interaction with God. However, there was a time when the answer was so clear that my reaction was, "Oh darn." I certainly felt that God had made His will known.

At another time I thought that God made His will perfectly clear also and that clarified a situation for me. But those were important things.

In the first example, I thought that the fleece that I chose would never happen, thereby allowing me to do what I wanted. God, however, answered the fleece doubly. Well, I guess He certainly let me know His will in that matter! In the second use of "the fleece" it was a matter of, I really do not want to do this, but I will, if you say so. No response to the fleece, which was good, but kept reminding God about the fleece, in case He changed His mind. (I don't know if God ever does that).

Somebody, I don't remember who, once said that God doesn't care about what you do. Well, I think my first example contradicts that theory; however, putting out the fleece willy nilly seems slightly deranged. I believe that that God looks over us with infinite love, respects our free will, and not only hears our prayers, but is aware of our every thought. Job said, "If I appealed to him and he answered my call, I could not believe that he would hearken to my words." But, I have been deeply touched when I have thought of something, not putting it into a request, and even my thought has been answered.

In addition, I have experienced a very special grace from God: I no longer struggle to forgive those who spread calumny about me. I am filled in mind, body and soul with deep compassion for them. Now when I pray for others, "Father, forgive them, for they know not what they do," I mean those words with my entire being and truly love each one of them. Only God could have given such a grace. And I am convinced that everything that comes into our lives comes by the will of God and is meant for our good, even those things that are extremely difficult to deal with.

I really believe, even in my "Stop the world, I want to get off" days, that there is nothing more beautiful than the will of God.

I am grateful to Bartholomew Schuler, Great grandfather Kessing, and all of my faith-filled ancestors for this precious treasure of the Catholic Faith. Their strength in enduring challenging lives with unwavering and steadfast belief in the truths of our religion has passed onto me a legacy that has incomparable value in this life and, most importantly, for eternity. I am confidant that they watch over us from that vantage point, pray for us, and look forward to our joining them in that happiness that has no words to express.

I have experienced that Our Lord has "come aboard" in the writing of these words. I give to Him whatever He wishes to make of the words I have written. I am including in this book two articles that I have written previously. The reason for including this first work, The Threshold of Eternity, is that I wrote it in the first days of my proceeding along a pathway new to me in the journey to God. I thought that there must be others on this journey, it could not be just for me.

And, I thought that it would be a comfort, an encouragement for others walking as I did to know that they were alone among the children of God on this same journey. So, I wrote this article, never before published, but which, I now hope will reach out to at least some of those others walking ever nearer to eternity.

THE THRESHOLD OF ETERNITY

After retirement from work it took a while before I was able to realize and appreciate that my days were now free from the pressure and tensions to which I had been accustomed. As my soul unfolded in the space of quietness and reflection, I began to experience God in my life a new and amazing way. Confident that I am not alone in this sacred journey that I dubbed the threshold of eternity, I have undertaken to share the whisperings of the Holy Spirit with all who treasure the life of faith above all that this transitory world has to offer.

One of the pitfalls of growing up in a faithful home is, I believe, that we have grown so accustomed to the familiar words and actions in community worship that we scarcely reflect on their meanings. Silence and time seem to allow the Holy Spirit to cast a new light and a deeper significance on the words, symbols, and actions of worship. In such a moment of quiet reflection, I was swept into silent awe as I remembered an almost overlearned catechism lesson. I recalled that, as children, we stood beside our desks as a sister quizzed us, each in turn, on questions from the catechism. In my memory, I heard again, "Why did God make you?" The response, "God made me to know him, to love him, and to serve him in this life and to be happy with him for all eternity," now began to fill me with a sense of wonder.

God's Plan for Us

God so designed us that we actually have the capacity to know him. He not only allows us to love him but made us for that very purpose. Our lives, our actions, our careers have a greater goal than to be successful; they provide us an opportunity to be in the service of Almighty God.

Over and over, I pondered this simple catechism statement. A more recent catechism is even more inspiring: "The ultimate end of the whole divine economy is the entry of God's creatures into the perfect unity of the Blessed Trinity." Even now, we are called to be a dwelling for the Most Holy Trinity: "If a man loves me," says the Lord, "he will keep my word, and my Father will love him, and we will love him, and we will come to him, and make our abode with him" (John 14:23).

At this point in this new journey, I was becoming aware that I was being given the grace of a deeper realization of the truths of our faith that I was being taught. As a consequence, my perspective on my life was being altered. This time of my life began to be very precious as I was led to puzzle over the mysteries of our faith and then to receive the responses to my pondering.

The answers to my questions came from the words of homilies at the Liturgy, from books, or from the words of others and began to lead me step by step to a greater depth of understanding of much that I thought I had known quite well.

Early in this new experience, I wondered, "Just what are going to be doing in eternity?" I found a wonderful answer in Pope Benedict XVI's *On the Way to Jesus Christ*.

In the writings of Gregory of Nyssa as well as Augustine, there are magnificent passages that set forth the infinitude of God's greatness and declare that all finding promotes further searching and that it will be our eternal joy to seek God's face—that is, to walk endlessly into the infinite in an ever new and joyful discovery and thus receive the adventure of eternal love as an answer to our thirst for happiness.

As the lessons began to unfold, I found that this precious time on earth is a prelude, a taste, a threshold of these delights. Eternity seen from the perspective of an "adventure of love" that became attractive, exciting, and inviting. In our life on earth, we are on the brink of that adventure. It then seemed to me that in the infinite longing that God has to share with us that adventure, he prepares us even now for eternal joy; he begins to reveal to us glimpses of the depths of mysteries that we will only learn more fully in the infinity that we call heaven.

God Made Us to Know Him

God reveals himself to us through Scripture, which unfolds for us in the Old Testament his faithful covenant with a persistent pursuit of his chosen people. However, mankind has set up repeated obstacles to God's desire to share his life with us. Our first parents abandoned intimacy with God to succumb to temptation; generation after generation turned away from God, and even the repeated punishments from God recounted in the Old Testament; again and again, the chosen people violated the covenant God had made with them. But God is steadfast in his love for man.

In the testing of Abraham when God asked him to sacrifice the son of promise, we catch a glimpse of the unwavering love that God has for mankind whom he created in order to share with them his life. The messenger of the Lord says to Abraham, "Do not do the least thing to him. I know how devoted you are to God, since you did not withhold from me your own beloved son" (Gen. 22).

Unfolding his eternal plan, God inspired the sacrifices of the Old Testament, the feeble offerings made by frail and sinful humans, to prefigure and prepare for the only sacrifice, which could redeem sinful man. Only God could repair the insult to God given by our sin. Only man could offer restitution for these sins. Inscrutable mystery of God's love— God did not withhold from us his own beloved Son. In his infinite love, the Father sent his Son so that God becoming man could redeem mankind. Above all, in Christ's sacrifice of himself in obedience to the Father, we behold the mystery of the Father's love for us. God told Abraham that he saw Abraham's love in that he was willing to sacrifice the son of promise. While God did not require the sacrifice from Abraham, God revealed his love for us by allowing or willing the passion and death of his beloved Son. The true sacrificial lamb, prefigured in the Passover ritual, is slain that sin might be forgiven and so we might live the life of God. This the price that we might enter the life of the Blessed Trinity.

God Made Us to Love Him and to Serve Him

Pope Benedict XVI gives us a poignant description of God's love for us. "In the pierced heart of the crucified, God's own heart is opened up—here we see who God is and what he is like.

Heaven is no longer locked up. God has stepped out of his hiddenness." But *why* does God love us? When God looks at us, he beholds something which is unimaginably loveable. He sees the creatures that he has made in his own image and likeness, that he has made to know him, to love him, and with whom he wants to share his life. In that love, we are bidden to love one another.

When we pray to be able to love others as God loves, what is it that we ask for? We are asking for the grace to look at others as God looks at them, to see beyond the flaws of personality, character deficits, even beyond mean and hurtful actions. We are asked to look at a person made in the image and likeness of God, made for the purpose of knowing God and loving God, made, as we are, to share the life of God. We are asked to love someone who has been bought at a great price. How then could we fail to love in union with God's loving? In loving service to others, we have the opportunity to respond to Christ's words, "Whatever you have done to the least of my brethren, you have to me" (Matt. 6:31). So great is God's love for each of us that he accepts our service of others as done to him.

God Made Us to Share His Life with Us

We share in the life of God by means of the Sacraments. The catechism tells us, "The Sacraments are efficacious signs of grace instituted by Christ, and entrusted to the Church, by which divine life is dispensed to us." Our sharing in the divine life began in the moment of Calvary when the Mystical Body of Christ came into being. We have the opportunity to participate in the life-giving surrender of Christ to his Father in the celebration of the Eucharist.

"The event of the Cross and Resurrection abides and draws everything toward life." Pope Benedict XVI tells us: "Today" embraces the whole time of the Church. And so in the Christian Liturgy, we not only receive something from the past but also become contemporaries with what lies at the foundation of the Liturgy.

By our prayerful participation in the Paschal mystery present in the Liturgical celebration, we enter into the life of the Son of God. He shares himself with us in the Eucharist that we might become one with him and with him surrender ourselves to the will of the Father.

Pope Benedict XVI tells us where God's will is done, there is heaven. There, earth becomes heaven. Surrendering ourselves to the action of God, so that we in turn may cooperate with him—that begins in the Liturgy and is meant to unfold further beyond it.

The God who created us to know him, to love him, and to serve him, who desires with infinite longing to share his life with us needs only our feeble cooperation in order to reveal himself to us. With St. Anselm, we pray eternity:

O God let me know you and love you so that I may find my joy in you, and if I cannot do so fully in this life, let me at least make some progress every day, until at last that knowledge, love and joy come to me in all their plentitude.

Growing in the knowledge and love of God of others makes this time the threshold of eternity.

TO BE SHARED

In this next section, I put forth an area that is very dear to my heart. It proceeds from the very words of Christ, therefore it is not "psychobabble," but has biblical authenticity. I referred to this concept in every one of the audiotapes that were produced by Alba House.

These are the very words of Christ from scripture:

Stop judging, that you may not be judged. For as you judge, so will you be judged, and the measure with which you measure will be measured out to you. Why do you notice the splinter in your brother's eye, but do not perceive the wooden beam in your own eye? How can you say to your brother, "Let me remove that splinter from your eye," while the wooden beam is in your eye? You hypocrite, remove the wooden beam from your eye first; then you will see clearly to remove the splinter from your brother's eye. (Matt. 7:1–6, NAB)

Carl Jung, whom a number of psychologists and psychiatrists disparage, does well in putting the judgmental thinking to which our Lord referred into his view of our psychological journey.

What I am now going to share with is something of great value (even financial value, as it is part of the groundwork presented by many professional psychologists and/or psychiatrists in private practice dedicated to personal growth).

The diagram on the next page is designed to clarify the Jungian view of the psyche—the conscious and the unconscious. The concept of the unconscious is actually possible to be demonstrated, not one of those strange ideas concocted by the erudite. Reputable diagnosticians have evaluated behaviors that give evidence of the physical existence of our unconscious.

Historically, there have been persons suffering from epileptic seizures that failed to respond successfully to medication. In 1960, attempting to arrive at control of these seizures, physicians performed surgery, corpus callosotomy, in which the two hemispheres in the brain were separated. Wikipedia records the work of Roger Sperry and Michael Gazzaniga in studying the behavior of the patients of this surgery. For example, a patient would be observed to be putting on his pants with one hand, while at the same time taking them off with the other. A woman would be seen putting an article away in a cupboard with one hand while taking it down with the other. The conclusion of the studies of such patients was that each hemisphere has a different function: one hemisphere that functions in a manner that is readily perceivable to the person and another that functions "unconsciously."

Somewhat related to that is Jung's theory that each one of us builds up what he calls a *persona*—a way of presenting ourselves that allows us to fit in and function in a way that is comfortable to ourselves in society. In doing so, we relegate the very opposite of that manner of presentation to our unconscious. The manner of speaking and acting that we have placed in our unconscious he calls our *shadow*.

However, the part of our psyche, the *persona*, seems to begin to fail us as we move into our midlife years. We begin to do and say things that we are uncomfortable about—a kind of "what made me say that?" "I never do things like that." But we have said it. We have done it.

In addition, Jung said that we not only deny factors in our personality, but because they are objectionable to our *persona*, we project these characteristics onto others. He paints a clear picture of how we know that we are doing this. We experience a strong emotional reaction to our perception of some fault that another person seems to us to be showing. We want to say to the other something like this: "Now sit down here, and I will tell what you are doing wrong, what you need to correct in yourself."

In other words, we really want to fix the other person. Now, Jung makes it clear that offending other person has a "hook," a small part of what troubles us.

That "hook" triggers our unconscious, alerting us to the fact that the fault that bothers us is really a fault in our personality.

The reason why I am intent on sharing this phenomenon with you is that I have found, for myself, that the Holy Spirit seems to use this human tendency to lead us to becoming "a new creation" in God's kingdom. This is how I have experienced the projection of my shadow onto another woman. (It's always another woman for a woman and another man for a man.) I become very disturbed by how another woman is acting. Even though I have "worked on" this projection hypothesis for many years, nevertheless, I find myself subject to projections. Carl Jung said that we never completely empty our unconscious of our shadow. In her description of the seven mansions of progress in the spiritual life, St. Theresa of Avila advised spiritual directors that they should never detain a person in any of the mansions except for the first mansion—the mansion of self-knowledge. She stated that no matter how much we progress in the spiritual life, we never leave the state of growing in self-knowledge.

That being said, I can expect to experience projections of my shadow and subsequent growth in self-knowledge as long as I live.

Everything is God's creation, including psychology.

There is another very helpful aspect of observing the phenomenon of projection. Other people project onto us and sometimes appear very upset in their need to "fix us." I have found that, while this very annoying, I can eliminate feelings of annoyance. First, I reflect on my words and actions (remembering that, after all, I am a "hook."). I ask for God's grace as I look within to find out if there is something that I need to change. Even when I cannot find, I know that there is a little feature of my personality that has triggered the other person's shadow, and I can forgive the other person in compassionate charity. Then I can really mean it when I say, "Father, forgive them for they not what they do."

I am including a paper that I wrote on the subject. I hope that will make the subject very clear.

11

THAT WE MIGHT GIVE GLORY TO GOD

She had not read the writings of learned authors, nor was she highly educated, but when my mother chastised me, as a child, with the words, "Take care, because when you point one finger at someone else, three fingers are pointed at yourself," she expressed the wisdom of saints and scholars. She gave a child the message of the scriptures, "Why do you notice the splinter in your brother's eye, but do not perceive the wooden beam in your eye?" (Matt. 7:3).

The saints admonish us to gain self-knowledge, which is the perception of the beam in our own eyes. In the *Dialogue of St. Catherine of Siena*, God the Father advises St. Catherine, "Never leave the knowledge of yourself. Then, put down as you are in the valley of humility, you will know me in yourself, and from this knowledge you will draw all that you need" (Catherine; *The Dialogue*, p. 29).

Steeped in simple wisdom, my mother's words showed the way to self-knowledge more than an admonition to "judge not," the words indicate, "Look, you have in yourself three times whatever it is that you are seeing in another." That seems very simple, but the search for genuine self-knowledge is a challenge to our minds darkened by the effects of original sin and our own personal sins. However, we can use a tool that psychology offers us to assist in this process. The concept of projection as developed by

Carl Jung helps us to face the daunting and painful task of courageously gaining self-knowledge. The search for humbling self-knowledge requires nothing more than to accept and explore the concept of projection—that is, we see in others what is, in fact, within ourselves. Jung called this "the shadow." Elements of our personalities that we have repressed are largely influenced by pressures of our environment and culture. However, these repressed and, for the most part, unconscious features of our personality, which we choose to disown, have a way of emerging. Other people come into our lives who "hook" these features within us. It is amazingly easy to notice these features in others, because we often find these people very disturbing. Sometimes, their presence alone is enough to upset us—words, actions, manner of dressing—any or all of these things annoy us. And our response is frequently, "But I *never* act like that."

We are *absolutely convinced* that we are, in fact, just the opposite from the people who offend us. That conviction comes from years of building within ourselves a misguided self-perception.

This inadequate and incomplete view of ourselves protects our ego, our pride. It allows us to reassure ourselves that we are just fine—"Not like the rest of humanity" (Luke 18:11).

There is no need to scour our souls with deep introspection in order to gain self-knowledge.

We only have to courageously find within ourselves what we so quickly project onto others. It is true, the qualities that we see in others are really there within them, but, as my wise mother indicated, only one-third as much as in ourselves. And, it is within ourselves that the Spirit of God desires to give us the treasure of self-knowledge. In granting us the grace of greater self-knowledge, the Holy Spirit leads us away from misperception to truth to our Lord—"The Way, The Truth, and the Life."

From the faith shown by a pioneer from Bohemia moving through years and given as a legacy to generations; the faith of a stowaway on board a ship handed down to me, to us, the faith in God that gives meaning to our lives; from that precious gift of faith, we open our minds and hearts to become a new creation. From the moment of the resurrection of our Lord and Savior, Jesus Christ, a new creation has begun. In our lives, we are being made a new creation. I hope and pray, as we are bidden by N.T. Wright, that these words may bring beauty into this world.

ACKNOWLEDGMENTS

First and above all, any good in this work is solely due to the Divine Author of all that is good, I have been absolutely overwhelmed at the graces that flowed to me in writing. Then, of course gratitude to his Mother, Seat of Wisdom, the recipient of everything that I am and have.

Then to the earthly angels who have played monumental roles in the formation of this narrative.

I offer my sincere gratitude to everyone who has not believed in me; each one by unwavering certitude of my guilt has been the tool of the Divine Artist, creating within me the reflection of God for which I have come into being. I shall be eternally grateful for that!

Without the generosity of Cindy Litten, Judy's sister, in driving me to places that I was unable to navigate, I would never have been able to undertake the project of The Chalice.

I treasure in my heart the gift that Joanne Lowe of Henninger's Church Goods Store has been, listening to my sobbing as I became aware of how painful it had been when, years ago, I was told that I was to leave the cloister. She was a rock of comfort as I became aware of the pain that I had kept deep within and only now allowed, what seemed like, an ocean of tears to fall. She was patient with me in those moments and a valuable assistant as I selected the chalice that would become the recipient of a master craftsman's artistic talent.

The experience of Master Jeweler Donald Kolick's helpfulness, receptivity, understanding, and kindness was something beyond anything that I could have asked for, or dreamed of. The artist jeweler, who remained nameless in a cloak of humility, produced a breathtakingly beautiful work of art.

While being overwhelmed in mourning of the loss of her son, Ann Laubenthal was a friend who not only listened to me, but who gave me a tremendous gift—her sincere assurance of respecting confidentiality. My confidence was greatly bolstered by the enthusiasm of Kim, Judy's niece, and Zachary, Kim's son. Equally supportive was Father Chuck's "awesome".

While the book is small, it has been one in which I have invested my very self. My hope and prayer is that it will, in deed, give glory to God.

REFERENCES

1. *Catechism of the Catholic Church*, 2nd ed. Washington DC: United States Catholic Conference, Inc., 1997) #260.
2. Benedict XVI. *On the Way to Jesus Christ.* San Francisco: Ignatius Press, 2005, 70.
3. Benedict XVI. *The Spirit of the Liturgy.* San Francisco: Ignatius Press, 2000, 48.
4. Catechism #1131.
5. *Ibid.* #1085.
6. Benedict XVI. *The Spirit of the Liturgy*, 57.
7. *Ibid.*, 176.
8. Anselm of Canterbury, from the *Proslogion*. (Quoted in The Liturgy of the Hours, II. New York: Catholic Publishing Corp.), 1775.

ABOUT THE AUTHOR

Maureen Schuler, PsyD, is retired from her most recent career of over twenty-five years as a clinical psychologist. In that profession, she had a series of audiotapes published. Prior to entering the field of psychology, she taught school at the grade school and junior high school level for twenty-five years. Her first career was a cloistered nun.

THE US REVIEW OF BOOKS

"For as long as I can remember, the Catholic faith was the cornerstone of our lives."

"As for any assault against yourself, consider that my will permits it to prove virtue in you and in my other servants. And assume that the offender does such a thing as an instrument commissioned by me. For often such a person's intention is good; there is no one who can judge the hidden heart."

—God the Father to St. Catherine of Siena

For over fourteen years, the author contemplated these words, trying to fit together how their message worked within the scope of her life experiences. Finally, she had a breakthrough realization: the bad things that happen to us are not just things that God allows to happen for our good, but those that he designs to happen to foster the creation within us of "His divine image." It is this realization that transformed an extremely painful experience in Schuler's life to one of beauty: "an awe-inspiring story of God's work of creation in my life." It is this story that Schuler feels compelled to reveal in her memoir, and she states that it is her "hope that this writing will be a manifestation of the beauty of God's creation."

Schuler begins her memoir by tracing both her paternal and maternal ancestries. Having lived through both world wars and the Great Depression, her parents were used to sacrifice and struggle. It was her mother who instilled in her the discipline of daily prayer by taking the author and her brother to daily Mass. From an early age, Schuler knew she wanted to be a nun. It was a dream from which she never wavered, and after her senior year of high school, she entered a cloistered community. Unfortunately, the experience wasn't a good one. Knowing very little about the workings of the kitchen, she was inept at the skills needed to be successful. After an unpleasant experience, she was sent home and joined another group where she was eventually assigned a teaching job.

There are some references to the life that Schuler led as a nun, though the brevity of the book leaves little room for expanding upon any one topic. Through the years, Schuler was placed in various teaching positions and was even allowed to help take care of her dying mother. After her mother's death and years into her career as a nun, she was seduced by an older nun who later lied about the incident and labeled Schuler as a sexual predator. She eventually received a degree in psychology and worked to understand this painful life experience.

This is an extremely touching book about betrayal and scandal. For example, when Schuler's seducer was questioned and laid the blame on the younger woman, not only did others believe the seducer, they shared the information with their group, leaving Schuler to face the accusations alone. The author writes honestly, boldly sharing her experience from a contemplative point of view. Having lived through the shame and sorrow of betrayal, she reached a place in her understanding of God's grace in her life from which she can truly embrace her relationship with her seducer as a lesson from God. In her book, Schuler candidly shows how she worked through her inner struggles to reach her conclusions, enabling her to explain them to her readers.

Though short in length, the book is heavy in substance. It is evident that the author has spent much time contemplating what happened to her and how to make sense of such a horrible experience. Having meditated on the words of God to St. Catherine led in part to her working out her feelings and sharing them in this book. Schuler's memoir is a fascinating work that is sure to evoke an emotional response in readers.

HOLLYWOOD BOOK REVIEWS

You Are a New Creation is a fascinating look at a nun's religious and personal discovery. Maureen Schuler has written an unforgettable book about her life as a nun. This book tells the story of Schuler's life as a nun with the Passionist nuns. She details the challenging tasks she had to perform as a novice nun. Schuler also writes about the joy she found teaching students as well.

However, Schuler's life changes forever after she has a sexual encounter with an older nun. The ensuing aftermath of that encounter led to her being ostracized by her religious community. In addition to her betrayal from her community, the encounter also leads her to struggle with her sexuality. Even though Schuler is presented with numerous challenges in her life, she finds faith in words from God to St. Catherine of Siena: "There is another thing you must do to attain this union and purity: You must never pass judgment in human terms on anything you see or hear from anyone at all, whether it concerns you or someone else. You must consider only my will for them and you."

Schuler's writing is confessional and heartbreakingly honest. When she writes about her betrayal by the nun that seduced her, readers will empathize with her wounded emotions. More remarkable is her ability to forgive after being shunned so publicly. Schuler's belief in forgiveness clearly comes from her resilient faith in God. Her writing about her renewal of her faith through her academic work and reading of Scripture also add depth to *You Are a New Creation*.

You Are a New Creation tells the story of Schuler's family history in Ohio as well. The beginning of the text details how her family immigrated to Ohio from Austria and Germany. Schuler also documents how her Catholic faith was passed down to her and how that faith guided her. The pictures of her family throughout the book add a personal touch to her memoir.

You Are a New Creation would be best for readers who want to learn more about the Catholic faith or want to delve more into faith if they're religious. Readers who like books about nuns' personal lives such as *Unveiled* by Cheryl L. Reed will also like this book as well. Even readers who aren't religious will be inspired by Schuler's forgiveness and perseverance through traumatic experiences.

You Are a New Creation shows how Schuler believes that God's grace helped her grow as a nun. Readers will be intrigued by this memoir of a life of service to a higher power.

www.ingramcontent.com/pod-product-compliance
Lightning Source LLC
Chambersburg PA
CBHW030159100526
44592CB00009B/354